Better Homes and Gardens®

two·color
Quilts

Meredith® Books
Des Moines, Iowa

Two-Color Quilts
Editor: Carol Field Dahlstrom
Writer: Susan M. Banker
Designer: Lyne Neymeyer
Publishing Copy Chief: Terri Fredrickson
Publishing Operations Manager: Karen Schirm
Edit and Design Production Coordinator: Mary Lee Gavin
Managers, Book Production: Pam Kvitne, Marjorie J. Schenkelberg, Rick von Holdt, Mark Weaver
Contributing Copy Editor: Arianna McKinney
Contributing Proofreaders: Julie Cahalan, Tricia Lawrence, Cindy McLeod
Technical Illustrator: Chris Neubauer Graphics, Inc.
Editorial and Design Assistant: Cheryl Eckert
Technical Editorial Assistant: Judy Bailey
Editorial Consultant: Jan Temeyer

Meredith® Books
Editor in Chief: Linda Raglan Cunningham
Design Director: Matt Strelecki
Managing Editor: Gregory H. Kayko
Executive Editor: Jennifer Dorland Darling

Publisher: James D. Blume
Executive Director, Marketing: Jeffrey Myers
Executive Director, New Business Development: Todd M. Davis
Executive Director, Sales: Ken Zagor
Director, Operations: George A. Susral
Director, Production: Douglas M. Johnston
Business Director: Jim Leonard

Vice President and General Manager: Douglas J. Guendel

Better Homes and Gardens® **Magazine**
Editor in Chief: Karol DeWulf Nickell

Meredith Publishing Group
President, Publishing Group: Stephen M. Lacy
Vice President-Publishing Director: Bob Mate

Meredith Corporation
Chairman and Chief Executive Officer: William T. Kerr

In Memoriam: E.T. Meredith III (1933–2003)

All of us at Meredith® Books are dedicated to providing you with information and ideas to create beautiful and useful projects. We welcome your comments and suggestions. Write to us at: Meredith Books, Crafts Editorial Department, 1716 Locust Street—LN120, Des Moines, IA 50309-3023.

If you would like to purchase any of our crafts, cooking, gardening, home improvement, or home decorating and design books, check wherever quality books are sold. Or visit us at: bhgbooks.com

The first vintage quilt I ever purchased was a two-color quilt. There was something about the graphic nature of the lovely red and white Tree of Life quilt that I couldn't resist. I was only 14 when I bought that quilt—it took most of my baby-sitting money and then some! I still have that quilt today and display it at Christmastime along with some of my other favorites.

Most of the vintage two-color quilts were made from the mid-1800s to about 1920. Contrary to what we might think, the women of that time did not always make their quilts from fabric scraps. Some quilt experts think that perhaps two-

color quilts were popular because only one other color than white needed to be purchased when designing the quilt. But the popularity of red and white and blue and white as the most significant two-color quilt themes also lends credibility to the idea that the centennial of 1876 made the colors of red, white, and blue very fashionable. It was around and after this time that most two-color quilts were made. Whatever the reason, we cherish these quilts as gorgeously graphic representational pieces of history.

Today, we continue to make two-color quilts for the same beautiful reasons as we did more than one hundred years ago. In this book of two-color quilts you'll find photographs and directions for making vintage-style quilts as well as more contemporary pieces using only two colors. In some cases we have given you some color options beyond two colors as well. Whatever your favorite style or color, we know you'll enjoy quilting these wonderful two-color quilts.

Carol Field Dahlstrom

contents

Because of their stark contrast and graphic nature, two-color quilts have been longtime favorites. They make a simple, direct statement and, therefore, blend easily into traditional and contemporary surroundings.

What are they? At their core, they are made from two fabrics, generally white and a color, which may be solid or print fabric. Only those two fabrics are used, and in their contrast and their simplicity, they seem to sparkle.

Around 1840 blue and white quilts became popular in America, often with detailed designs. Bright red and white quilts also were a favorite choice. Part of the popularity of the two combinations, of course, was because of the permanence of the dyes.

Many quilters were known to have a blue and white quilt in their collections, with an indigo and white quilt sometimes being considered the best of the collection. Historians figure that is why so many quilts of that color combination survived: They were special, and, therefore, not used on a daily basis. Indigo was considered a superior dye because it produced a color that was true and fast. With demand so high, companies printed large quantities of the blue fabrics.

While many of the two-color blue and white quilts featured some appliqué designs, most were pieced, which tended to show off the striking color combination.

Indigo blue and turkey red were reliable dyes, another reason the fabric combinations were popular. Indigo blue tends to be a rich, deep blue, although Prussian or Lafayette blue and light blue also were used. Turkey red and other shades, including a variety of pinks and dark roses, also were common.

In pieced blue and white quilts, popular pieced patterns included Mariner's Compass and Feathered Star, and later in the 1800s, Drunkard's Path and Bow Tie. In appliquéd versions, leaves and floral designs topped the list.

In dating blue and white quilts, historians often look to the white fabric for clues. From 1875 through 1925, printed white shirting fabric is common. Earlier quilts often featured plain white cotton. If the blue is lighter, in the pastel range, the quilt likely is from the 20th century.

The blue and white popularity extended to woven coverlets made during the same time frame. In fact, some quilts seem to have been inspired by the Jacquard designs in the coverlets, with intricate geometric center designs and floral borders.

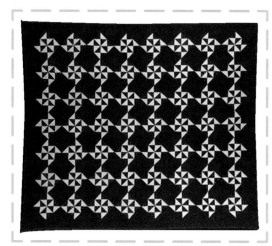

Pinwheel
c. 1880–1900

Maker unknown. Courtesy:
University of Nebraska-Lincoln,
No. 1997.007.0452

Turkey red and white quilts also have been classics since the 1840s. At about the same time, green color schemes were popular for quilts too. General color taste, availability of fabrics, and most importantly, the colorfastness of the red cotton likely contributed to the combination.

During the mid-19th century, the red fabrics used were both plain and printed. After about 1875, the reds were more often solid. The stark contrast of red and white showed off patterns using leaf, star, and fleur-de-lis motifs. Toward the end of that century, red and white were the most common choices for pieced patterns, such as Sawtooth, Ocean Wave, and Schoolhouse.

Turkey red, with its enduring colorfastness, remained so popular because new synthetic dyes were often unreliable. The same was true for red cotton embroidery thread, which was used for redwork embroidered quilts.

By the early 20th century, prints got lighter, brighter, and cheerier. A bluish red replaced turkey red. Simple blue vat dyes replaced indigo dyed blues. Germany's aniline dye formulas gave more depth of color. Greens and yellows became brighter, and pastels improved greatly. Purple and black became reliable colors.

It's truly amazing how changes in fabrics follow history. Just imagine what history your quilts will hold.

Album
c. 1908–1914

Made in Monmouth County, New Jersey, this quilt has multiple signatures. Courtesy: University of Nebraska-Lincoln, No. 1997.007.0252

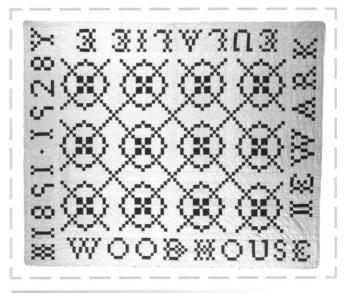

Burgoyne Surrounded
c. 1891–1928

Made in Newark, New York, by Eulalie E. Woodhouse. Courtesy: University of Nebraska-Lincoln, No. 1997.007.0485

Red and white was a favorite color combination used in quilts during the mid-1800s.  Turkey red, time-tested and colorfast, was widely used. Today collectors treasure the classic red and white patchwork designs for the clean look and sturdy construction.

twirling patchwork
The graphic elements of this antique quilt offer multiple layout possibilities. By changing the color placement and rotating the units, you can achieve several lovely looks. Complete instructions are on pages 46–49.

blooming lattice

Challenge your sewing creativity with this historical block that officially remains nameless. The block center, a Nine-Patch variation, is surrounded by an unusual triangle unit. See multicolor variations of this striking pattern on page 15.

materials

3½ yards of red pindot for
    blocks and binding
2½ yards of white pindot
    for blocks
2⅝ yards of muslin for sashing
    and borders
5½ yards of backing fabric
79×96" quilt batting

Finished quilt: 71¾×89½"
Finished block: 12" square

Quantities specified for 44/45"-wide 100% cotton fabrics. All measurements include a ¼" seam allowance unless otherwise stated.

cut the fabrics

To make the best use of your fabrics, cut the pieces in the order that follows.

To make templates of Patterns D, E, F, G, and H, on *page 14*, follow the instructions in Quilter's Primer beginning on *page 179*. No pattern pieces are designated for A, B, and C; these letters are for placement only.

For this project the border strips are cut the length of the fabric (parallel to the selvage). This list includes mathematically correct border strip lengths. You may wish to add extra length to the strips now to allow for sewing differences later.

From red pindot, cut:
- 4–2½×96" binding strips
- 20–5⅛" squares, cutting each diagonally twice in an X for a total of 80 triangles, or 80 of Pattern H (page 14)
- 40–3⅜" squares, cutting each diagonally twice in an X for a total of 160 triangles, or 160 of Pattern G (page 14)
- 128–2" squares for Position A
- 32–3¼" squares for Position C
- 80 of Pattern D (page 14)
- 80 of Pattern F (page 14)

From white pindot, cut:
- 288–2×3¼" rectangles for Position B
- 160 of Pattern E (page 14)

From muslin, cut:
- 2–3¾×65¾" border strips
- 2–3¾×90" border strips
- 31–6¼×12½" sashing strips

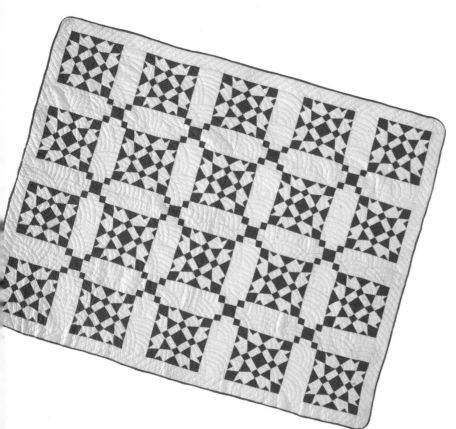

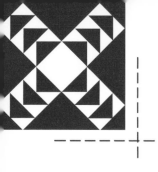

blooming lattice continued

assemble the units

Unit A

1. For one Unit A you'll need four red pindot A squares, one red pindot C square, and four white pindot B rectangles.

2. Referring to Diagram 1, sew a red pindot A square to opposite ends of a white pindot B rectangle to make a small pieced rectangle. Press seam allowances toward the red squares. Repeat to make a second small pieced rectangle.

Diagram 1

3. Join a white pindot B rectangle to opposite edges of the red pindot C square (see Diagram 2) to make a large pieced rectangle. Press the seam allowances toward the red square.

Diagram 2

4. Join the pieced rectangles as shown in Diagram 3 to make one Unit A. The pieced unit should measure 6¼" square, including the seam allowances.

Diagram 3
Unit A
Make 32 of Unit A

5. Repeat Steps 1 through 4 to make a total of 32 of Unit A; set aside 12 of Unit A.

Unit B

1. For one Unit B you'll need two white pindot B rectangles, two white pindot E triangles, one red pindot D triangle, one red pindot F piece, and two red pindot G triangles.

2. Referring to Diagram 4, sew together one red pindot D triangle and one white pindot E triangle. Press the seam allowance toward the red triangle. Join the remaining white pindot E triangle with the red pindot F piece. Press the seam allowance toward the red piece. Sew together one white pindot B rectangle and one red pindot G triangle. Press the seam allowance toward the red triangle. Repeat to make a reverse piece as shown.

Diagram 4
Unit B
Make 80 of Unit B

3. Sew together the sections to make one Unit B.

4. Repeat Steps 1 through 3 to make a total of 80 of Unit B.

Unit C

1. For one Unit C you'll need one Unit B and two red pindot H triangles.

2. Referring to Diagram 5, sew a red pindot H triangle to the side edges of Unit B to make one Unit C.

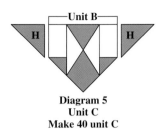

Diagram 5
Unit C
Make 40 unit C

3. Repeat Steps 1 and 2 to make a total of 40 of Unit C.

assemble the blocks

1. For one block you'll need one Unit A, two Unit Bs, and two Unit Cs.

2. Referring to the Block Assembly Diagram for placement, lay out the pieces for one block. First sew a Unit B to opposite side edges of Unit A. Press seam allowances toward Unit A. Then join a Unit C to the top and bottom edges of Unit B/A/B to make a block. Press the seam allowances toward Unit B/A/B. The pieced block should measure 12½" square, including the seam allowances.

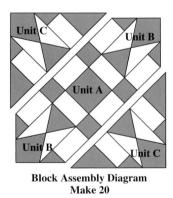

Block Assembly Diagram
Make 20

3. Repeat Steps 1 and 2 to make a total of 20 blocks.

assemble the quilt top

1. Referring to the photograph, *page 10*, for placement, lay out the 20 blocks and 15 of the 6¼×12½" muslin sashing strips in five horizontal rows, alternating the blocks and sashing strips in each row. Each block row should begin and end with a block. Join the pieces in each row. Press the seam allowances toward the muslin sashing strips. Each pieced block row should measure 12½×65¾", including the seam allowances.

2. Lay out the remaining 12 of Unit A and the remaining 16 of the 6¼×12½" muslin sashing strips in four horizontal rows, alternating the units and sashing strips in each row. Each Unit A row should begin and end with a sashing strip. Join the pieces in each row. Press the seam allowances toward the muslin sashing strips. Each pieced Unit A row should measure 6¼×65¾", including seam allowances.

3. Sew together the horizontal rows, alternating block rows with Unit A rows. The top and bottom rows should be block rows. Press the seam allowances toward the Unit A rows. The pieced quilt top should measure 65¾×83½", including the seam allowances.

assemble the borders

Sew one 3¾×65¾" muslin border strip to the top edge and one to the bottom edge of the pieced quilt top. Press the seam allowances toward the muslin borders. Join one 3¾×90" muslin border strip to each side edge of the quilt. Press the seam allowances toward the muslin borders.

complete the quilt

Layer the quilt top, batting, and backing according to the instructions in Quilter's Primer beginning on *page 179*. Quilt as desired. The antique quilt shown on

here's a tip

Use dense allover prints for small pieces because they tend to blend with the motifs of sparse prints and look like solids. Also use small allover prints for backing and to camouflage seams and quilting lines.

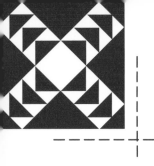

blooming lattice continued

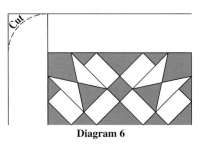

Diagram 6

page 11 was hand-quilted with an allover fan shape.

Using a compass or a pencil and a round saucer, mark a round shape in each quilt corner (see Diagram 6). Trim on marked line. Bind the quilt with red pindot binding strips, following instructions in Quilter's Primer.

here's a tip

If you want the quilt to cover your pillows, measure the mattress length, then add one drop length plus 10" to 20" for the pillow tuck. The exact amount to add will depend on the pillow size and depth of your tuck.

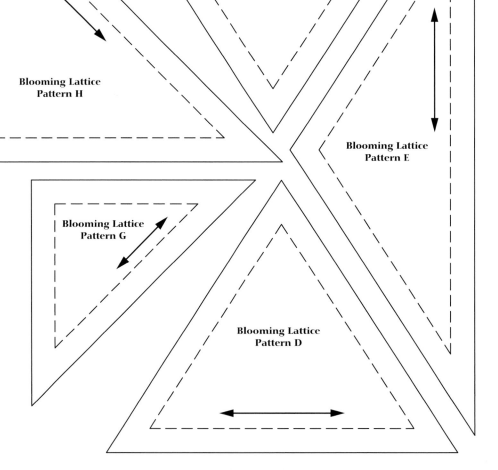

Blooming Lattice Pattern F

Blooming Lattice Pattern H

Blooming Lattice Pattern E

Blooming Lattice Pattern G

Blooming Lattice Pattern D

Make a Multicolor Version of This Two-Color Quilt

Blooming Lattice blocks look different with subtle design changes and drastically different fabric and color choices.

To achieve the dramatic look, *top right,* use vibrant fabrics against a dark background. The quilt pattern is modified with simple squares replacing each pieced Unit A. These add dots of color on the black strips.

For a quieter version, *bottom right,* choose reproduction fabrics for a vintage look. This sample combines blue and mauve fabrics with a white small print.

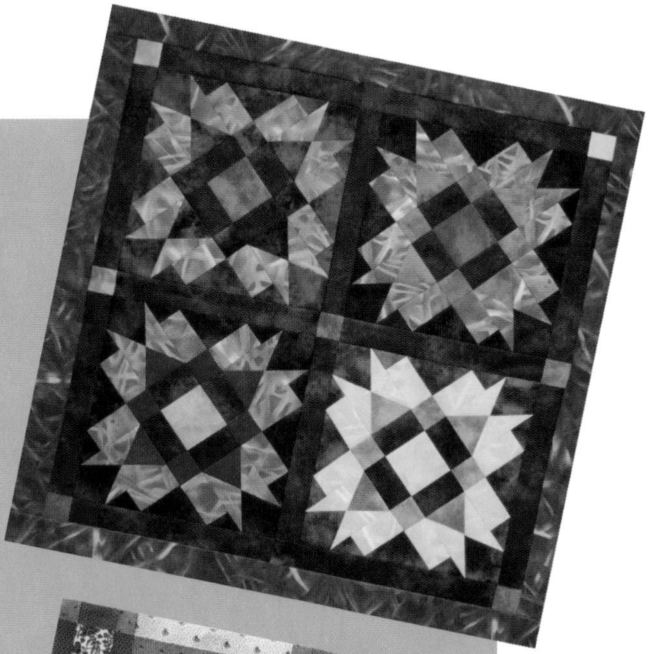

optional sizes for Blooming Lattice

To make other sizes, use this information for dimensions and yardages.

Quilt Sizes	Table Runner	Wall	King
Number of Sashing Blocks	0	9	25
Number of Blocks	3	4 (2×2)	36 (6×6)
Final Size	18½×42½"	41¾" square	107¼" square
Red pindot	1 yard	1¼ yards	5½ yards
White pindot	¾ yard	¾ yard	4¼ yards
Muslin	1⅛ yards	1⅝ yards	3⅛ yards
Backing	1¼ yards	1⅔ yards	9½ yards
Batting	20×60"	42" square	113" square

robbing peter to pay paul

In the 1800s, quiltmakers wanted to name their new blocks and often chose names to commemorate important people or events. This is how the Robbing Peter to Pay Paul block also came to be known as Dolley Madison's Workbox.

materials

6 yards each of white and red fabrics
5¾ yards of backing fabric
90×108" precut quilt batting
Template material

Finished quilt: 68×96"
Finished block: 7" square

designer notes

This block appears to be pieced, but the curves are actually achieved by appliquéing four melon-shape pieces (A) onto a solid fabric square.

cut the fabrics

To make a template of Pattern A, *page 19,* follow the instructions in Quilter's Primer beginning on *page 179.*

From white fabric, cut:
• *1—20×108" strip (from this strip, cut four 2½×108" border strips and four 2½×80" border strips)*
• *48—7½" squares*
• *192 of Pattern A*

here's a tip
Quilters use the term "quilt sandwich" to describe the quilt top, batting, and backing once they've been layered together.

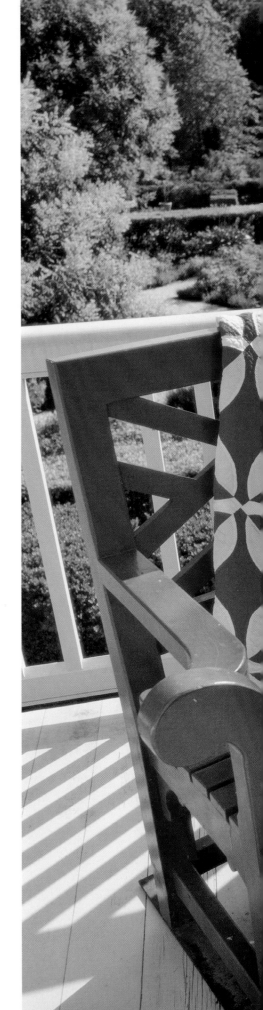

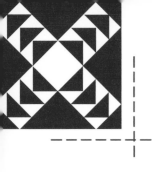

robbing peter to pay paul continued

From red fabric, cut:
- *1—10×108" strip (from this strip, cut two 2½×80" border strips and two 2½×108" border strips)*
- *1—8×98" strip for straight-grain binding*
- *48—7½" squares*
- *192 of Pattern A (page 19)*

assemble the blocks

1. On each A piece, turn under the seam allowance on the curved edge only. Clip the seam allowance if necessary to achieve a smooth curve; press or baste the seam allowance in place, if desired. Leave the straight edge flat (it is sewn into the seam when adjacent blocks are joined).

2. Align the straight edge of one white A piece with one edge of a red square. Approximately ¾" should show above and below the white A piece on the straight edge. Appliqué the curved edge to the red fabric.

3. Appliqué a white A piece onto each of the three remaining sides of the red square in the same manner.

4. Repeat, sewing four white A pieces onto each red square and four red A pieces onto each white square. Make 48 blocks of each color combination.

assemble the quilt top

1. Join the blocks into 12 horizontal rows of eight blocks each, alternating red and white squares, to make six rows that begin with a red square and six rows that begin with a white square.

2. Join rows, alternating rows and carefully matching seam lines. The assembled quilt top should measure approximately 56×84".

assemble the borders

1. Match two white border strips with one red strip of the same length. Stitch the strips together lengthwise with the red one in the center. Assemble four white/red/white borders.

2. Sew long border sections onto the sides of the quilt top; sew the short sections at the top and bottom sides. See Quilter's Primer beginning on *page 179* for instructions to miter border corners.

complete the quilt

Layer the quilt top, batting, and backing according to the instructions in Quilter's Primer. Quilt as desired. The quilt shown on *pages 16–17* is outline quilted ¼" out around each A piece and the border seams.

See Quilter's Primer to make and apply binding. Cut approximately 332" inches of red fabric for binding.

here's a tip

Both stencils and templates are patterns. A template is a pattern created by marking around a shape. A stencil is a pattern through which a design is transferred. Stencils have slits in the surface for you to mark through them, while a template's outer edge is in the shape of its design.

You can make your own stencils and templates or purchase them ready-made at a quilt shop.

Quilt Assembly Diagram

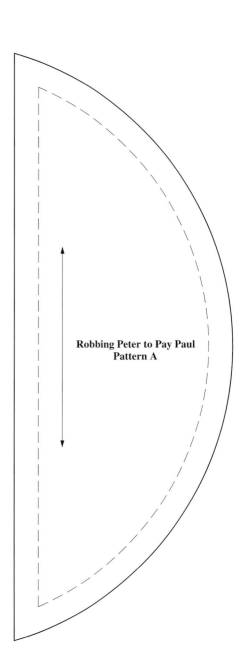

**Robbing Peter to Pay Paul
Pattern A**

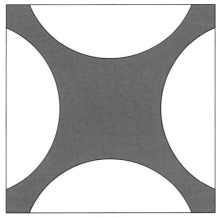

Quilt Block

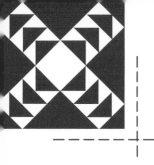

delectable mountains

Peaked mountains radiate
from the center square of
this majestic quilt. Simple straight
quilting enhances
the dramatic design.

materials

3 yards of red cotton fabric
3½ yards of white cotton fabric
¾ yard of red cotton fabric for binding
4¾ yards of backing fabric
80" square quilt batting
Template material, graph paper, pencil, scissors

Finished quilt: approximately 74" square

designer notes

Add ¼" seam allowances to all pattern
pieces. Whenever possible, press seams
toward red fabric to prevent red
seams from showing through on the
white pieces.

prepare the patterns

Draw the following shapes onto graph
paper: For Template A, draw a 9-inch
square; diagonally divide the square in
half to create the triangle for Template C.
Divide Triangle C in half for Template B.
Template E is a right triangle with 12" legs.
Make templates from each of these shapes.

Trace and transfer the full-size patterns
for Templates D and F, *page 23*, to template
material. Cut out the templates.

here's a tip

If you're assembling
a quilt on a table
that is smaller than
the quilt backing,
center the fabric on
the table top so
equal lengths hang
down on each side
like a tablecloth.

delectable mountains continued

cut the fabrics

The E triangles are cut with the long side on the straight of the fabric grain; all other triangles are cut with the legs on the straight of the fabric grain.

From red fabric, cut:
- *1 of Pattern A*
- *24 of Pattern C*
- *168 of Pattern D (page 23)*
- *104 of border Pattern F (page 23)*

From white fabric, cut:
- *16 of Pattern E*
- *20 of Pattern C*
- *4 of Pattern B*
- *168 of Pattern D (page 23)*
- *104 of border Pattern F (page 23)*

assemble the blocks

1. Sew a B triangle to each side of A. Sew a red C to each of the four sides to complete center square.
2. Sew together the white C triangles and remaining red C triangles along the long side to form 20 squares. Piece eight pairs of C squares along the white sides to make eight rectangles. Four red and white squares remain.
3. Sew pairs of E triangles into four large triangles for corners.
4. Sew red D triangles and white D triangles together to form squares.
5. Refer to the Quilt Assembly Diagram, *opposite*, to assemble diagonal rows. Sew the rows together, repeating Rows 2, 3, and 4 on the opposite side of Row 1 to complete the top.

assemble the borders

1. Sew together pairs of red and white F triangles to make squares. Make two borders, each with 25 squares; sew the borders to opposite sides of the quilt top. Make two borders, each with 27 squares; sew the borders to the remaining opposite sides of the quilt.

complete the quilt

1. Layer the quilt top, batting, and backing according to the instructions in Quilter's Primer, *page 179*. Quilt as desired. Quilting all D and E triangles creates a delightful appearance. Quilt parallel lines or fancy quilting designs in each of the larger triangles.
2. From the binding fabric, cut eight 3×44" strips. Follow the instructions in Quilter's Primer to bind the quilt.

here's a tip

If you're basting a quilt on a small table or in limited space, consider thread-basting the batting and backing together before basting the quilt top into the quilt sandwich. This extra step will give you better control and help prevent shifting as you baste all three layers.

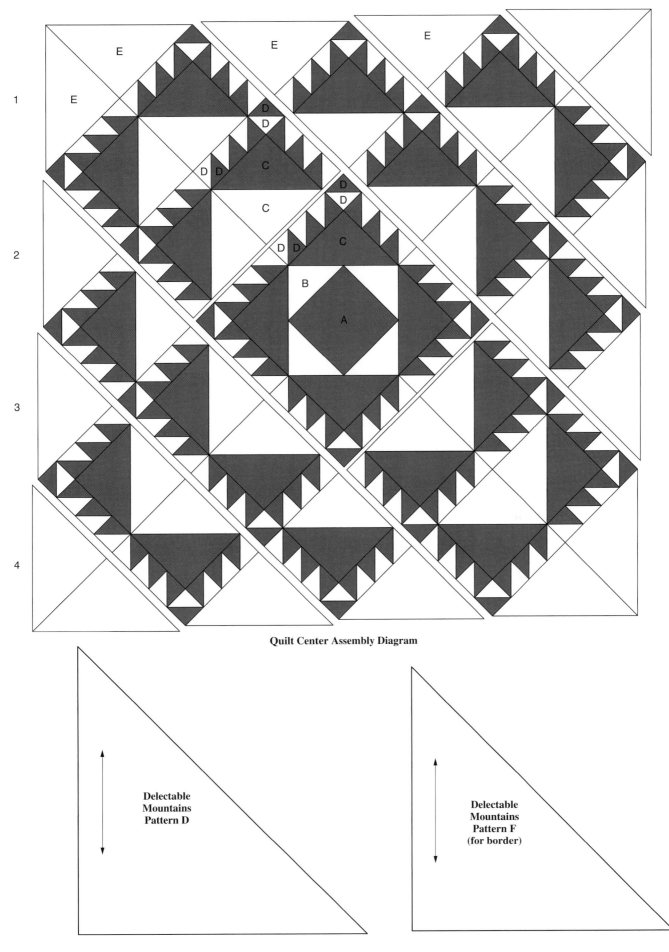

Quilt Center Assembly Diagram

Delectable Mountains Pattern D

Delectable Mountains Pattern F (for border)

toyland redwork sampler

Redwork, a form of embroidery that uses red thread to outline-stitch simple line drawings, was popular from the late 1880s through the 1930s. Recently, a new following, which uses the technique to re-create revived patterns, has developed.

 **pattern sheet**

history of redwork

During the mid-1880s redwork embroidery was brought to America from Europe, where it was called turkey work. The technique uses outline or stem stitch to embroider line drawings. Originally, such items as flowers, animals, and people (oftentimes from magazines) were traced or transferred to white background squares for stitching.

Stitchers sometimes embroidered preprinted muslin penny squares, so called because they sold for a penny. Stitched squares often were set side by side and featherstitched together with red thread to make summer coverlets.

materials

2¾ yards of white print for blocks
and borders
¾ yard of large red polka-dot print for
blocks and borders
¾ yard of small red polka-dot print for
blocks and borders
¼ yard each of 9 assorted red prints
for blocks and borders
3 yards of backing fabric
52×64" quilt batting
Red embroidery floss; embroidery hoop
Pigma pen–permanent red fine-tip

Finished quilt: 46×58"
Finished blocks: 6" square

Quantities specified are for 44/45"-wide 100% cotton fabrics. All measurements include a ¼" seam allowance unless otherwise stated.

cut the fabrics

To make the best use of your fabrics, cut the pieces in the order that follows. For this project, cut the border strips the length of the fabric (parallel to the selvage). You may add extra length to border strips now to allow for sewing differences later.

From white print, cut:

- *1–20×42" rectangle for*
  embroidery foundation
- *2–2½×46½" strips for middle border*
- *2–2½×38½" strips for middle border*
- *24–2½×6½" rectangles*

- *62–2½" squares*
- *15–2½×17" strips*
- *42–2⅞" squares*

From large red polka–dot, cut:

- *3–2½×42" binding strips*
- *48–2½" squares*
- *4–2⅞" squares*

From small red polka–dot, cut:

- *3–2½×42" binding strips*
- *48–2½" squares*
- *6–2⅞" squares*

From assorted red prints, cut:

- *12–2½×17" strips*
- *32–2⅞" squares*
- *50–2½" squares*

assemble nine-patch blocks

1. Aligning long raw edges, sew together one 2½×17" white print strip and one 2½×17" red print strip. Sew a second 2½×17" red print strip to the opposite long edge of the white print strip to complete Strip Set A (see Diagram 1). Press seam allowances toward the red print strips. Repeat for a total of three of Strip Set A.

   Cut the strip sets into a total of eighteen 2½"-wide segments.

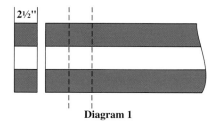

Diagram 1

2. In the same manner, sew a 2½×17" white print strip to each long edge of a 2½×17" red print strip to make Strip Set B (see Diagram 2). Press seam allowances toward the red print strip. Repeat for a total of six of Strip Set B.

Cut the strip sets into a total of thirty-six 2½"-wide segments.

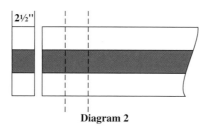

Diagram 2

3. Lay out one Strip Set A segment and two Strip Set B segments as shown in Diagram 3. Sew together the rows to make a Nine-Patch block. Press the seam allowances in one direction. The pieced Nine-Patch block should measure 6½" square, including seam allowances.

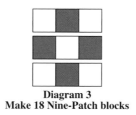

Diagram 3
Make 18 Nine-Patch blocks

4. Repeat Step 3 to make a total of 18 Nine-Patch blocks.

embroider the squares

1. Starting in the upper left corner of the 20×42" white print embroidery foundation rectangle (about 1" from the edges), use a quilting pencil to lightly mark 17 adjoining 6½" squares. Do not cut the squares apart.

2. Center and trace one of the nine embroidery designs on the Pattern Sheet to each square using the red fine-tip permanent Pigma pen. The project shown on *page 25* uses eight of the designs twice and one design once.

3. Use an outline stitch and two strands of red floss to embroider the designs, using an embroidery hoop to keep the fabric taut.

4. After you complete the stitched embroidery, cut apart the squares on the drawn lines.

assemble the blocks

1. For accurate sewing lines, use a quilting pencil to mark a diagonal line on the wrong side of 34 of the 2½" small red polka-dot squares and 34 of the 2½" large red polka-dot squares. (To prevent fabric from stretching as you draw lines, place 220-grit sandpaper beneath the squares.)

2. For one embroidered block, you'll need two marked small red polka-dot squares, two marked large polka-dot squares, and one embroidered square.

3. Right sides together, align one small red polka-dot square with one corner of the embroidered square (see Diagram 4; noting the sewing line placement). Stitch on the sewing line. Trim the seam

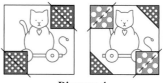

Diagram 4

here's a tip

The best fabric for quiltmaking is 100-percent cotton. Cotton fabric minimizes seam distortion, presses crisply, and is easy to quilt.

allowance to ¼". Press open the attached small red polka-dot triangle.

4. In the same manner, sew a second small red polka-dot square to the opposite corner of the embroidered square; trim and press open.

5. Repeat with the two large red polka-dot squares and the remaining two corners of the embroidered square; trim and press.

6. Sew the remaining polka-dot squares to the remaining 16 embroidered squares.

assemble the quilt top

Referring to the photograph, *page 29*, lay out the 18 Nine-Patch blocks and the 17 embroidered blocks in seven horizontal rows of five blocks each, alternating the blocks. Sew together the blocks in each row. Press the seam allowances toward the embroidered blocks. Join the rows. Press the seam allowances in one direction. The pieced quilt top should measure 30½×42½", including the seam allowances.

assemble the inner borders

1. For accurate sewing lines, use a quilting pencil to mark a diagonal line on the wrong side of 14 of the 2½" small red polka-dot squares and 14 of the 2½" large red polka-dot squares.

2. Raw edges aligned, place a marked small red polka-dot square on the left end of six of the 2½×6½" white print rectangles (see Diagram 5; noting sewing line placement). Stitch on the marked sewing line. Trim the seam to ¼". Press open the attached small red polka-dot triangle. Stitch a marked large red polka-dot square to the opposite end of each rectangle in the same

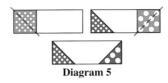

Diagram 5

manner; trim and press to make a rectangle unit.

3. To make the top inner border strip, you'll need three rectangle units from Step 2 and two 2½×6½" white print rectangles.

4. Lay out the rectangles in a horizontal row, beginning and ending with a rectangle unit. Sew together the rectangles. Press the seam allowances toward the white print rectangles. The pieced top inner border should measure 2½×30½", including seam allowances. Sew the pieced inner border strip to the top edge of the pieced quilt top.

5. Repeat Steps 3 and 4 to make the bottom inner border strip; sew to the bottom edge of the pieced quilt top.

6. Raw edges aligned, place a marked large red polka-dot square on the left end of eight of the 2½×6½" white print rectangles. Stitch on the marked sewing line; trim and press. Sew a marked small red polka-dot square to the opposite end of each rectangle; trim and press to make a rectangle unit.

7. For a side inner border strip, you'll need four rectangle units from Step 6, three 2½×6½" white print rectangles, and two 2½" white print squares.

8. Lay out the rectangles in a vertical row, beginning and ending with a 2½" white print square. Join the pieces. Press the seam allowances toward the white print pieces. The pieced side inner border strip should measure 2½×46½",

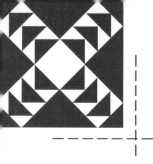

toyland redwork sampler continued

including seam allowances. Sew to one side edge of the pieced quilt top.

9. Repeat Steps 7 and 8 for a second side inner border strip; sew to the remaining side edge of the pieced quilt top.

assemble middle borders

1. Sew a 2½×46½" white print middle border strip to each side edge of the pieced quilt top. Press seam allowances toward the white print middle border.

2. Sew one 2½×38½" white print middle border strip to the top edge and one to the bottom edge of the pieced quilt top. Press the seam allowances toward the white print middle borders. The pieced quilt top should measure 38½×50½", including seam allowances.

assemble outer borders

1. For accurate sewing lines, use a quilting pencil to mark a diagonal line on the wrong side of six of the 2⅞" small red polka-dot squares, four of the 2⅞" large red polka-dot squares, and 32 of the 2⅞" assorted red print squares.

2. Raw edges aligned, join each marked 2⅞" red print and polka-dot square to a 2⅞" white print square, sewing ¼" on each side of the marked center line (see Diagram 6). Cut apart on the marked

line to make red and white triangle-squares. Press seam allowances toward the red print triangle. Each pieced triangle-square should measure 2½" square, including seam allowances. Repeat to make a total of 84 triangle-squares.

3. For the top outer border strip, you'll need 18 red and white triangle-squares, 11 of the 2½" white print squares, and nine of the 2½" assorted red print squares.

4. Referring to Diagram 7, lay out the squares in two rows, noting the placement of the triangle-squares.

5. Sew together the squares in each row. Join the rows. The pieced top outer border strip should measure 4½×38½", including seam allowances. Join the top outer border strip to the top edge of the pieced quilt top.

6. Repeat Steps 3 through 5 for the bottom outer border strip; join to the bottom edge of the pieced quilt top.

7. For a side outer border strip, you'll need 24 red-and-white triangle-squares, 18 of the 2½" white print squares, and 16 of the 2½" assorted red print squares.

8. Referring to Diagram 8, lay out the squares in two rows, noting the placement of the triangle-squares.

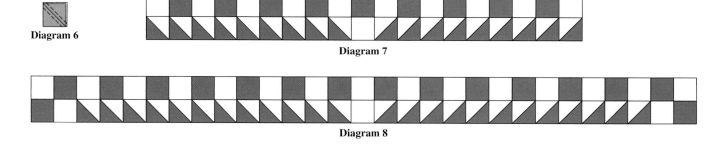

Diagram 6

Diagram 7

Diagram 8

9. Sew together the squares in each row. Join the rows. The pieced side outer border strip should measure 4½×58½", including seam allowances. Join the side outer border to one side edge of the pieced quilt top.

10. Repeat Steps 7 through 9 to make a second side outer border strip; join to remaining side edge of pieced quilt top.

complete the quilt

Layer the quilt top, batting, and backing according to the instructions in Quilter's Primer beginning on *page 179*. Quilt as desired. The quilt on *page 25* is machine-quilted diagonally through the Nine-Patch blocks, extending into the borders. Use the 2½×42" large red polka-dot and small red polka-dot strips to bind the quilt, following instructions in Quilter's Primer.

here's a tip

To avoid having embroidery floss colors bleed onto fabrics, prewash and dry the floss.

toyland redwork pillow

materials

⅜ yard of white print
⅛ yard of red plaid
¾ yard of large red polka-dot
¼ yard of small red polka-dot
⅛ yard of red stripe
½ yard of large red check
24×30" of muslin
24×30" of thin quilt batting
Red embroidery floss
1 package of red jumbo rickrack
Pigma pen—red fine-tip permanent
Quilting pencil
9—¾"-diameter red buttons

Finished case: fits standard 20×26"
or 20×28" pillow form

cut the fabrics

To make the best use of fabrics, cut the pieces in the order that follows.

From white print, cut:
• *1—14½×8½" rectangle for embroidery foundation*
• *2—2×21" strips*

From red plaid, cut:
• *2—1½×14½" strips*
• *2—1½×8½" strips*

From large red polka-dot, cut:
• *2—5¾×16½" strips*
• *2—16½×21" rectangles*
• *2—2½" squares*

From small red polka-dot, cut:
• *2—4¼×21" strips*
• *2—2½" squares*

From red stripe, cut:
• *2—1½×21" strips*

here's a tip

Although it's easy to get absorbed in quilting, it's important to your health to pause for a few minutes every hour. Step away from your sewing machine or quilting frame and stretch. You'll be revitalized.

From large red check, cut:
• *1—18" square, cutting it into enough 2½"-wide bias strips to total 100" length*

From jumbo rickrack, cut:
• *4—23" lengths*

embroider the blocks

1. Trace three embroidery designs from the Pattern Sheet onto the 14½×8½" white print rectangle, using the red pen and placing designs to clear the fabric edges by at least 1" all around.

2. Use an outline stitch and two strands of red floss to embroider the designs.

assemble the blocks

1. For accurate sewing lines, use a quilting pencil to mark a diagonal line on the wrong side of the two 2½" small red polka-dot squares and the two 2½" large red polka-dot squares.

2. Align one small red polka-dot square with one corner of the embroidered rectangle; sew, trim, and press.

3. In the same manner, sew a second small red polka-dot square to the opposite corner of the embroidered square; trim and press.

4. Repeat with the large polka-dot squares and the remaining corners of the embroidered rectangle; trim and press.

5. Sew one 1½×8½" red plaid strip to each side edge of the embroidered rectangle. Sew one 1½×14½" red plaid strip to the top edge and one to the bottom edge of the embroidered rectangle to complete the center rectangle. Press seam allowances toward the red plaid strips.

assemble the borders

1. Sew one 5¾×16½" large red polka-dot strip to the top edge of the center rectangle and one to the bottom edge. Press seam allowances toward the large red polka-dot strips.

2. Sew one 1½×21" red stripe strip to each side edge of the center rectangle. Press seam allowances toward the red stripe strips.

3. Baste a 23"-length of jumbo rickrack to the right side of each long edge of a 2×21" white print strip, centering the rickrack along the ¼" seam allowance and starting the rickrack at the same point in the wave on each side of the strip. Repeat on the second 2×21" white print strip.

4. Sew one white print strip to each side edge of the center rectangle. Press seams toward the red stripe strips.

5. Sew one 4¼×21" small polka-dot strip to each side of the center rectangle to complete the pieced pillow top. Press seam allowances toward the small polka-dot strips.

quilt the pillow top

Layer the pillow top, batting, and muslin backing according to instructions in Quilter's Primer, beginning on *page 179*. Quilt as desired. Baste together the outside edges through all layers ¼" from the raw edge. Trim batting and backing even with the quilted pillow top. Using a small plate as a template, curve the corners of the pillow top. Baste corners ¼" from the raw edges. Sew three buttons along each narrow white strip.

complete the pillow

1. Turn under 1" along one long edge of each 16½×21" large polka-dot rectangle; press. Turn under again 1"; press. Using matching thread, stitch through all layers close to the second folded edge.

2. Vertically center and stitch three buttonholes in the hemmed edge of one of the rectangles. Center and sew three buttons, to correspond with the buttonholes, along the hemmed edge of the opposite rectangle. Button the rectangles together for the pillow back.

3. Wrong sides together, pin the pillow top to the pillow back. Using the 2½"-wide large red check bias strips, bind the pillow, following instructions in the Quilter's Primer.

here's a tip
If you take a quilting class, you may see BSK on the supply list. This abbreviation represents "basic sewing kit," which consists minimally of scissors, needles, and thread.

red double-X

Each Double-X block requires three different fabrics. To re-create the scrappy yet organized look of this quilt, mix as many as five different prints for a few blocks.

materials

12–⅓-yard pieces of assorted red prints for blocks

12–⅓-yard pieces of assorted cream prints for blocks

3½ yards of red floral for setting squares, setting triangles, and corner triangles

¾ yard of cream and red print for inner borders

2¼ yards of red stripe for outer border and binding

8 yards of backing

104×95"of quilt batting

Finished quilt: 97½×88½"

Finished block: 6" square

Quantities specified are for 44/45"-wide 100% cotton fabrics. All measurements include ¼" seam allowances. Sew with right sides together unless otherwise stated.

cut the fabrics

To make the best use of fabrics, cut them in the order that follows.

The setting and corner triangles are cut slightly larger than necessary; trim them to the correct size after piecing the quilt top.

From *each* of 12 assorted red prints, cut:

- *23–2⅞" squares, cutting each in half diagonally for a total of 46 triangles (you'll have 12 triangles leftover)*
- *4–2½" squares (you'll have 6 squares left over)*

From each of the 12 assorted cream prints, cut:

- *23–2⅞" squares, cutting each in half diagonally for a total of 46 triangles (you'll have 12 triangles leftover)*
- *19–2½" squares*

From red floral, cut:

- *9–12" squares, cutting each diagonally twice in an X for a total of 36 setting triangles (you'll have 2 triangles leftover)*
- *2–8½" squares, cutting each in half diagonally for a total of 4 corner triangles*
- *72–6½" squares*

From cream and red print, cut:

- *9–2×42" strips for the inner border*

From red stripe, cut:

- *9–4¼×42" strips for the outer border*
- *10–2½×42" binding strips*

assemble double-X blocks

1. To make Double-X Block A, you need six triangles from one red print, six triangles from one cream print, and three 2½" squares from a second cream print.

2. Sew together one cream print triangle and one red print triangle to make a triangle-square (see Diagram 1). Press the seam allowance toward the red print triangle. The pieced triangle-square should measure 2½" square, including seam allowances. Repeat to make a total of six triangle-squares.

Diagram 1

red double-X continued

3. Referring to Diagram 2 for placement, lay out the triangle-squares and three 2½" cream print squares in three horizontal rows. Sew together the pieces in each row. Press seam allowances in one direction, alternating the direction with each row. Join the rows to make a Double-X Block A. Press seam allowances in one direction. The pieced Double-X Block A should measure 6½" square, including seam allowances.

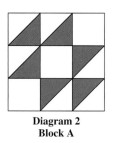

**Diagram 2
Block A**

4. Repeat Steps 1 through 3 to make a total of 48 of Double-X Block A.

5. To make Double-X Block B, you'll need six triangles from one red print, six triangles from one cream print, two 2½" squares from a second cream print, and one 2½" square from a second red print.

6. Referring to Diagram 3 and following steps 2 and 3, make a Double-X Block B.

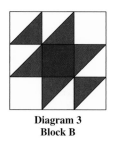

**Diagram 3
Block B**

7. Repeat Steps 5 and 6 to make a total of 42 of Double-X Block B.

here's a tip
To avoid having the entire quilt beneath the sewing-machine arm at one time, begin working at the center of a quilt and work toward one edge. Complete half of the quilt top, then turn it around and quilt the other half, keeping in mind any directional motifs you may be stitching.

assemble the quilt center

1. Refer to the Quilt Assembly Diagram, *opposite*, and lay out the Double-X blocks, the 72 red floral setting squares, and 34 red floral setting triangles in diagonal rows.

2. Sew together the pieces in each diagonal row. Press seam allowances in each row toward the setting squares and triangles. Join the rows. Press seam allowances in one direction.

3. Sew on the four red floral corner triangles to complete the quilt center. Press seam allowances toward the red floral corner triangles.

4. Trim the pieced quilt center to measure 78½×87", leaving 1" beyond the Double-X block corners.

assemble the borders

The following border measurements are mathematically correct. You may cut the strips longer than specified to allow for possible sewing differences.

1. Cut and piece the 2×42" cream and red print strips to make the following:
- 2–2×90½" inner border strips
- 2–2×78½" inner border strips

2. Sew the short cream and red print inner border strips to the side edges of the quilt center. Sew the long cream and red print inner border strips to the top and bottom edges of the quilt center. Press all seam allowances toward the inner borders.

3. Cut and piece the 4¼×42" red stripe strips to make the following:
- 2–4¼×98" outer border strips
- 2–4¼×81½" outer border strips

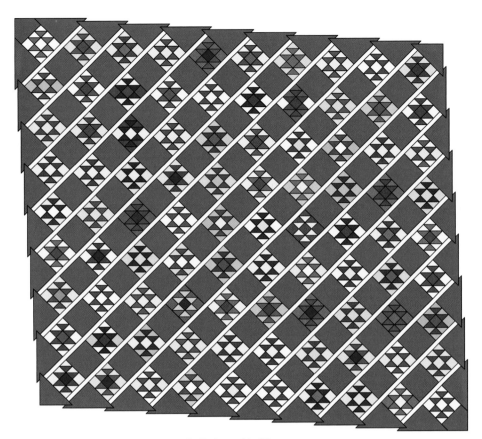

Quilt Assembly Diagram

here's a tip
Some machine quilters wear special gloves with grippers on the palms for better control as they shift the quilt on the machine bed when quilting.

4. Sew the short red stripe outer border strips to the sides of the quilt center. Sew the long red stripe outer border strips to the top and bottom edges of the quilt center to complete the quilt top. Press all seam allowances toward the outer borders.

complete the quilt
1. Layer the quilt top, batting, and backing following instructions in Quilter's Primer, beginning on *page 179*. Quilt as desired.

2. Use the 2½"-wide red stripe strips to bind the quilt following instructions in Quilter's Primer.

PILLOW SHAMS
materials for two
¾ yard of white and red print for front
1¼ yards of 110"-wide muslin or
 2⅜ yards of 42"-wide muslin for
 lining and backing
1⅛ yards of red print for scalloped flange
1¾ yards of lightweight sew-in interfacing

Finished sham: 26½×32½"
(fits a standard size bed pillow)

cut the fabrics
To make the best use of fabrics, cut the pieces in the order that follows. Patterns are on the Pattern Sheet.

 pattern sheet

red double-X continued

From white and red print, cut:
- 2—19½×25½" *rectangles*

From muslin, cut:
- 4—21½×27" *rectangles*
- 2—19½×25½" *rectangles*

From red print, cut:
- 4 of Pattern A *(Pattern Sheet)*
- 4 of Pattern B *(Pattern Sheet)*

From lightweight interfacing, cut:
- 4 of Pattern A *(Pattern Sheet)*
- 4 of Pattern B *(Pattern Sheet)*

assemble the fronts

1. Right sides up, layer a 19½×25½" white and red print rectangle on a 19½×25½" muslin rectangle. Machine-baste along all four sides ⅛" from the edges to make the pillow sham front.

2. Layer each red print A piece and red print B piece on a corresponding interfacing piece; pin. Layer the flange pieces on the pillow sham front. Sew together, beginning and ending seams ¼" from each end. Press the seam allowance toward the red print flange.

3. Right sides together, diagonally fold the pillow sham front to align the two angled corner edges of the A/B flanges (see Corner Assembly Diagram). Join the two pieces with a ¼" seam allowance; press the seam allowance open. Complete the

remaining three corner flange seams in the same manner to make a pillow sham front with a flange.

4. Repeat Steps 1 through 3 to make a second pillow sham front with a flange.

complete the pillow shams

1. Stitch a double ¼" hem along one long edge of two 21½×27" muslin rectangles. Overlap the hemmed edges by 5". Stitch across the folds ⅛" from the top and bottom edges to secure the pieces, creating a pillow sham back.

2. Right sides facing, layer the pillow sham front on the pillow sham back. Pin layers together every 2½". Sew the pieces together around the entire pillow sham front. Trim excess muslin to ³⁄₁₆" beyond the seam. Notch the outer curves and clip the inner curves.

3. Turn the pillow sham right side out, making sure flange edges are full and rounded; press.

4. Working on a hard, smooth surface, pin through all layers in the ditch created where the flange meets the white-and-red print sham front.

5. Stitch-in-the-ditch around the white-and-red print sham front, backstitching at the two places where the pillow sham back hems intersect with the stitching line to strengthen the sham at its greatest stress points.

here's a tip

To avoid force-feeding a quilt into a sewing machine, feed the fabric up to the walking foot gently, but don't push the fabric ahead. Pushing it causes tucks at the crossing of each seam. Try not to stretch the quilt top or force it under the needle as that will cause the batting to pull, which will distort the finished quilt.

Corner Assembly Diagram

6. Repeat Steps 1 through 5 to make a second pillow sham.

BUTTON-BAND PILLOW
materials

⅜ yard of red floral for pillow front and back
⅓ yard of red stripe for pillow front
¼ yard of cream and red print for pillow band
3–1"-diameter cream buttons
12×16" pillow form

Finished pillow: 12×16"

cut the fabrics

To make the best use of fabrics, cut the pieces in the order that follows.

From red floral, cut:
• *1–13×17" rectangle*
• *1–6¾×13" rectangle*

From red stripe, cut:
• *1–10¾×13" rectangle*

From cream–and–red print, cut:
• *1–7×13" rectangle*

assemble the pillow

1. Sew together the 6¾×13" red floral rectangle and 10¾×13" red stripe rectangle to make the pillow front. The pieced pillow front should measure 13×17", including seam allowances.

2. To make the band, right sides together, fold the 7×13" cream and red print rectangle in half lengthwise to make a 3½×13" strip. Sew together the long edges of the strip; turn right side out and press. Turn the seam to the center of one side.

3. Right sides facing up, center the band over the front seam of the pillow front. Machine-baste in place along the raw

edges. Position the buttons on the band; stitch them only to the band.

4. Layer the pieced pillow front and 13×17" red floral pillow back. Sew around the outer edges, leaving an opening to accommodate the pillow form along one end, to make the pillow cover. Turn the pillow cover right side out. Insert the pillow form through the opening. Whipstitch the opening closed.

PIECED PILLOW
materials

⅜ yard total of assorted red prints for blocks and binding
⅜ yard of cream print for blocks and pillow back
14½" square of muslin
14½" square of batting
12"-square pillow form

Finished pillow: 12" square

here's a tip
Let the large work surface around your sewing machine support the weight of the quilt as you machine-quilt. Avoid letting the quilt drop to the floor and create drag. If you have a limited work surface, adjust an ironing board to the height of your sewing machine bed to help support the quilt's weight.

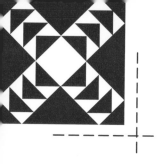

red double-X continued

cut the fabrics

To make the best use of fabrics, cut the pieces in the order that follows.

From assorted red prints, cut:
- *2–2½×28" binding strips*
- *2–6½" squares*
- *6–2⅞" squares, cutting each in half diagonally for a total of 12 triangles*

From cream print, cut:
- *2–12½×10½" rectangles*
- *6–2½" squares*
- *6–2⅞" squares, cutting each in half diagonally for a total of 12 triangles*

assemble the pillow front

1. Referring to Assemble Double-X Blocks instructions beginning on *page 32*, follow Steps 1 through 3 to make two of Double-X Block A. The pieced blocks should measure 6½" square, including seam allowances.

2. Referring to the Assembly Diagram, lay out the two Double-X blocks and the two 6½" red print squares in rows.

3. Sew together the pieces in pairs. Press seam allowances toward the red squares. Join the pairs to make the pillow front. Press seam allowances in one direction.

4. Layer the pieced pillow front, the 14½" batting square, and the 14½" muslin square. Machine- or hand-quilt as desired. The featured pillow was quilted in evenly spaced diagonal rows.

Assembly Diagram

complete the pillow

1. Press under ¼" along a long edge of each 12½×10½" cream print rectangle. Press under an additional 2"; stitch in place to hem the pillow back pieces.

2. Wrong sides together, pin the two pillow back pieces to the pillow front, aligning raw edges and overlapping folded edges. Sew together along all four sides to make the pillow cover.

3. Use the 2½"-wide red print strips to bind the pillow cover, following instructions in Quilter's Primer, beginning on *page 179*. Insert the pillow form.

ENVELOPE PILLOW pattern sheet
(shown on *page 37*)

materials

1¼ yards of white and red print for pillow front, flap lining, and pillow back
⅜ yard of red print for pillow flap
1–1¼"-diameter cream button
18"-square pillow form

Finished pillow: 18" square

cut the fabrics

To make the best use of fabrics, cut the pieces in the order that follows. The pattern is on the Pattern Sheet.

From white-and-red print, cut:
- *2—19×24" rectangles*
- *1—19" square*
- *1 of Pattern A (Pattern Sheet)*

From red print, cut:
- *1 of Pattern A (Pattern Sheet)*

assemble the pillow front

Note: Use a ½" seam allowance.

1. To make the flap, sew together the white and red print and red print Pattern A pieces, stitching between the large dots marked on the pattern. Trim the seams and clip the curves. Turn right side out and press.

2. Right sides up, place the flap on the 19" white-and-red print square. Machine-baste ¼" along the edges to secure the flap. Stitch the button to the flap, stitching through the pillow top.

complete the pillow

1. Wrong sides facing, fold the 19×24" white and red print rectangles in half to form two 12×19" double-thick pieces. Overlap the folded edges by 4". Stitch across the folds ½" from the top and bottom edges to secure the pieces and complete the pillow back. *Note:* Two layers give the pillow back stability.

2. With right sides together, layer the pillow front and pillow back. Sew together along all four edges to make the pillow cover. Turn the cover right side out; insert the pillow form.

HANDKERCHIEF VALANCE
materials

4—⅛-yard pieces of assorted red prints for blocks
4—⅛-yard pieces of assorted cream prints
    for blocks
4—2½" squares of assorted dark red prints
    for blocks
⅓ yard of white and red print for triangles
1 yard of red floral for triangles
¼ yard red stripe for rod pocket
1½ yards of muslin for lining

Finished valance: 13×76"
Finished block: 6" square

cut the fabrics

To make the best use of fabrics, cut the pieces in the order that follows.

From each of the 4 assorted red prints, cut:
- *3—2⅞" squares, cutting each in half diagonally for a total of 6 triangles*

From each of the 4 assorted cream prints, cut:
- *3—2⅞" squares, cutting each in half diagonally for a total of 6 triangles*
- *2—2½" squares*

From white and red print, cut:
- *2—12" squares, cutting each diagonally twice in an X for a total of 8 triangles*

From red floral, cut:
- *3—15" squares, cutting each in half*

red double-X continued

diagonally for a total of 6 triangles
(you'll have one leftover triangle)

From red stripe, cut:

- *2—4×42" strips*

From muslin, cut:

- *5—15" squares, cutting each in half diagonally*
  for a total of 10 triangles (you'll have one
  triangle leftover)
- *2—4×42" strips*

assemble the blocks

1. Referring to Assemble Double-X
Blocks instructions beginning on
page 32, follow Steps 5 through 6 to
make a Double-X Block B. The pieced
block should measure 6½" square,
including seam allowances.

2. Repeat to make a total of four
Double-X Block B.

assemble the valance

1. Referring to Diagram 1, sew a
white and red print triangle to adjoining
edges of a Double-X block to make a
pieced triangle. Repeat to make a total
of four pieced triangles.

2. Right sides together, layer a pieced
triangle and a muslin triangle. Stitch
together on the two short sides (see
Diagram 2). Turn right side out and
press to make a lined pieced triangle.
Repeat to make a total of four lined
pieced triangles.

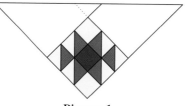

Diagram 1

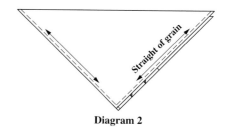

Diagram 2

3. In the same manner, sew together a red
floral square and a muslin square to
make a lined red square. Turn right side
out and press. Make a total of five lined
red squares.

4. Lay out the lined pieced triangles and
the lined red squares in a row,
overlapping them as shown (see
Diagram 3, *opposite*). Stitch together
along the long, straight edge to make
the pieced valance unit. The pieced
valance unit should measure 88" long
across the long edge.

5. Piece the 4×42" red stripe strips end to
end. (*Note:* The resulting red stripe strip
will be shorter than the pieced valance
unit.) Right sides together, center the red
stripe strip along the long edge of the
pieced valance unit; stitch in place.
Press the seam allowance toward the
red stripe strip.

6. Piece the 4×42" muslin strips end to
end. (*Note:* The resulting muslin strip
will be shorter than the pieced
valance unit.) Sew the muslin strip to
the raw edge of the red stripe strip;
press the seam allowance toward the
red stripe strip.

7. Cut off the ends of the valance at 77½".
Turn under ¼" at each end; press. Turn

here's a tip

When washing quilts,
choose a cleaning
agent that is safe
for quilts. Laundry
detergents are harsh
on cotton quilts, and
they accelerate the
wear of fabrics.

under ½" at each end; press and stitch to hem.

8. Press under ¼" of the unfinished edge of the muslin strip. Fold the muslin to the back of the valance to cover the seam line. (*Note:* The seam joining the red stripe and muslin strips should be invisible.)

9. Working from the valance front, edge-stitch on the red stripe strip next to the seam line, joining the strip to the lined triangles. Make sure the muslin hem on the reverse side is caught in the stitching to form the rod pocket.

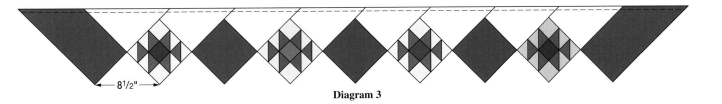

Diagram 3

8½"

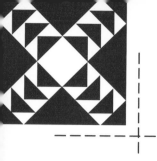

pinwheel swirl

This classic quilt is a jewel, alive with contrast and movement. To call attention to the star shape formed around the square in each block, cut the square from the same fabric as you cut the points.

materials

4¼ yards of muslin for blocks, sashing, and borders

5⅜ yards of solid red for blocks, sashing, and binding

4⅞ yards of backing fabric

73×87" of quilt batting

Finished quilt: 67×81"

Finished block: 4" square

Quantities specified are for 44/45"-wide 100% cotton fabrics. All measurements include a ¼" seam allowance unless otherwise stated.

cut the fabrics

To make the best use of your fabrics, cut the pieces in the order that follows.

From muslin, cut:
- *8–2×42" border strips*
- *546–2½" squares*
- *143–3⅜" squares*

From solid red, cut:
- *8–2½×42" binding strips*
- *273–2½×4½" rectangles*
- *130–2½" squares*
- *286–2⅞" squares, cutting each in half diagonally for a total of 572 triangles*

assemble the blocks

1. For one block, use one 3⅜" muslin square and four solid red triangles.

2. Right sides together, align the long edge of a solid red triangle with one edge of the muslin square (see Diagram 1).

Sew together the pieces. Press the seam allowance toward the solid red triangle. In the same manner, align a second solid red triangle with the opposite edge of the muslin square; join and press.

Diagram 1
Make 143 blocks

3. Sew the two remaining solid red triangles to remaining opposite edges of the muslin square. The pieced block should measure 4½" square, including seam allowances.

4. Repeat Steps 1 through 3 to make a total of 143 blocks.

assemble the sashing units

1. For accurate sewing lines, use a quilter's pencil to draw a diagonal line on the wrong side of each 2½" muslin square. (To prevent fabric from stretching as you draw the lines, place 220-grit sandpaper beneath the squares.)

2. For one sashing unit, you'll need one 2½×4½" solid red rectangle and two 2½" muslin squares.

3. Right sides together, align a muslin square with one end of the solid red rectangle (see Diagram 2; note the placement of the marked diagonal line). Stitch on the marked line; trim the seam allowance to ¼". Press the attached triangle open.

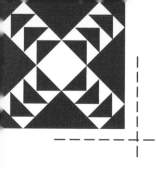

pinwheel swirl continued

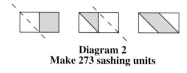

Diagram 2
Make 273 sashing units

4. Right sides together, align the second muslin square with the opposite end of the solid red rectangle (see Diagram 2; noting placement of the marked diagonal line). Stitch on the marked line; trim and press to complete the sashing unit. The pieced sashing unit

should measure 2½×4½", including seam allowances.

5. Repeat Steps 1 through 4 to make a total of 273 sashing units.

assemble the rows

1. For a block row, you'll need 11 blocks and 10 sashing units.
2. Refer to Diagram 3 on *page 45* and lay out the pieces in a horizontal row. Sew together the pieces. Press seam

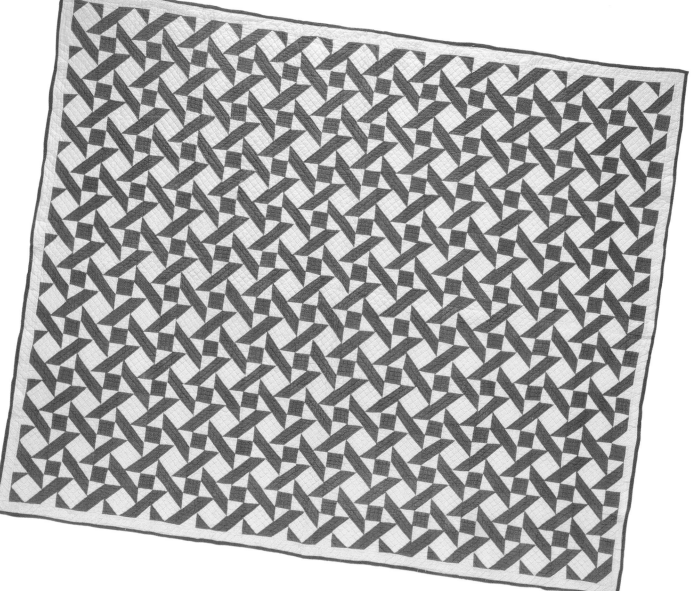

allowances toward the blocks. The pieced block row should measure 64½×4½", including seam allowances.

3. Repeat Steps 1 and 2 to make a total of 13 block rows.

4. For a sashing row, use 11 sashing units and 10 of the 2½" solid red squares.

5. Refer to Diagram 4 and lay out the pieces in a horizontal row. Sew together the pieces to make a sashing row. Press seam allowances toward the solid red squares. The pieced sashing row should measure 64½×2½", including seam allowances.

6. Repeat Steps 4 and 5 to make a total of 13 sashing rows.

assemble the quilt top

Referring to the photograph, *opposite*, lay out the block and sashing rows. Sew together the rows to make the quilt top. Press seam allowances in one direction. The pieced quilt top should measure 64½×78½", including seam allowances.

assemble the border

1. Cut and piece the 2×42" muslin strips to make the following:
  • 2–2×78½" border strips
  • 2–2×67½" border strips

2. Sew one 2×78½" muslin border strip to each side edge of the pieced quilt top. Sew one 2×67½" muslin border strip to the top and one to the bottom of the pieced quilt top. Press seam allowances toward the muslin borders.

complete the quilt

Layer the quilt top, batting, and backing according to instructions in Quilter's Primer, beginning on *page 179*. Quilt as desired. Use the 2½×42" solid red strips to bind the quilt, following instructions in Quilter's Primer.

here's a tip
Having extra fabrics on hand when working on projects presents opportunities for substitutions and variety in piecing quilts. When you buy a variety of fabrics, you'll enjoy playing with the combinations to achieve new and varied results for a multitude of quilt designs.

Diagram 3
Make 13 block rows

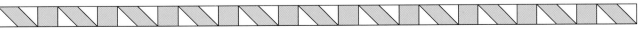

Diagram 4
Make 13 sashing rows

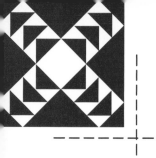

twirling patchwork

The graphic elements of this block offer multiple layout possibilities. Try rotating the block to create an entirely different look.

here's a tip

Pair neutral colors, such as beige or cream, with a multicolor print. In the midst of color, neutral pieces give the eye a place to rest. They also divide the competing colors and increase contrast.

materials

6⅞ yards of red print for blocks, borders, and binding
5½ yards of muslin for blocks
5⅔ yards of backing fabric
72×102" of quilt batting

Finished quilt: 66×96"
Finished block: 10" square

Quantities specified are for 44/45"-wide 100% cotton fabrics. All measurements include ¼" seam allowances. Sew with right sides together unless otherwise indicated.

cut the fabrics

To make the best use of fabrics, cut the pieces in the order that follows. The pattern pieces are on *page 49*. To make templates, follow instructions in Quilter's Primer, beginning on *page 179*.

From red print, cut:
• 8–3½×42" border strips
• 9–2½×42" binding strips
• 108–2⅞" squares, cutting each in half diagonally for a total of 216 triangles, or 216 of Pattern C (page 49)
• 216 of Pattern A (page 49)
• 216 of Pattern B reversed (page 49)

From muslin, cut:
• 108–2⅞" squares, cutting each in half diagonally for a total of 216 triangles, or 216 of Pattern C (page 49)
• 216 of Pattern A reversed (page 49)
• 216 of Pattern B (page 49)

assemble the blocks

1. Referring to Diagram 1 for placement, sew together one red print A piece, one muslin B piece, and one red print C triangle to make a Subunit A. Press seam allowances toward the red print pieces. Repeat to make a total of 216 of Subunit A.

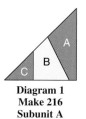

Diagram 1
Make 216
Subunit A

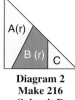

Diagram 2
Make 216
Subunit B

2. Referring to Diagram 2, sew together one muslin A reversed piece, one red print B reversed piece, and one muslin C triangle to make a Subunit B. Press the seam allowances toward the red print piece. Repeat to make a total of 216 of Subunit B.

3. Sew together one Subunit A and one Subunit B to make a quarter unit (see Diagram 3). The pieced quarter unit should measure 5½" square, including seam allowances. Repeat to make a total of 216 quarter units.

Diagram 3
Make 216 quarter units

4. Referring to Diagram 4, lay out four quarter units in two rows. Sew together the units in each row. Press seam allowances in opposite directions. Join the rows to make a block. Press the seam allowance in one direction. The pieced block should measure 10½" square, including seam allowances.

5. Repeat Step 4 to make a total of 54 blocks.

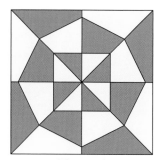

Diagram 4
Make 54 blocks

assemble the quilt center

1. Referring to the photograph on *page 46* for placement, lay out the 54 blocks in nine horizontal rows. Sew together the blocks in each row. Press seam allowances in one direction, alternating the direction with each row.

2. Join the rows to complete the quilt center. Press seam allowances in one direction. The pieced quilt center should measure 60½×90½", including seam allowances.

assemble the borders

1. Cut and piece the 3½×42" red print strips for the following:
- 2–3½×60½" border strips
- 2–3½×96½" border strips

2. Sew a 3½×60½" red print border strip to the top and bottom edges of the pieced quilt center. Sew a 3½×96½" red print border strip to each side of the pieced quilt center to complete the quilt top. Press seam allowances toward the red print borders.

complete the quilt

1. Layer the quilt top, batting, and backing according to instructions in Quilter's Primer, beginning on *page 179*.

2. Quilt as desired. The antique quilt in the photograph was hand-quilted ¼" inside the edges of each piece.

3. Use the 2½×42" red print strips to bind the quilt, following instructions in Quilter's Primer.

here's a tip

Evaluate an antique quilt before attempting to clean it. Improper cleaning damages quilts. If a quilt has sentimental or monetary value, consult an expert.

optional sizes for Twirling Patchwork

To make other sizes, use this information for dimensions and approximate yardages. Yardage is based on the number of blocks indicated and a sashed border that is similar to the original quilt.

Quilt Size	Lap	Queen	King
No. of Blocks	12 (3×4)	72 (8×9)	121 (11×11)
Finished size	36×46"	86×96"	116" square
Red print	2½ yards	8⅞ yards	13¾ yards
Muslin	1½ yards	7⅛ yards	11⅔ yards
Backing	1½ yards	7⅔ yards	10 yards
Batting	42×52"	92×102"	120" square

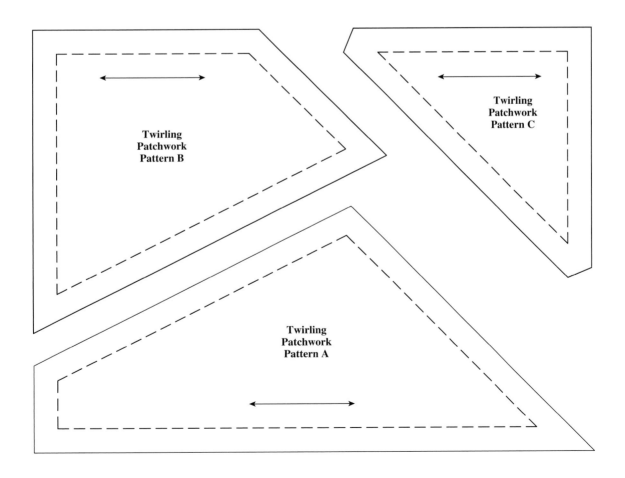

Twirling
Patchwork
Pattern B

Twirling
Patchwork
Pattern C

Twirling
Patchwork
Pattern A

king solomon's temple

The striking combination of solid red and solid white in this traditional pattern makes a royal statement of splendor. To achieve similar results, select two fabrics with high contrast.

materials

3¾ yards of muslin for blocks and borders

4⅛ yards of solid red for blocks, borders, and binding

4½ yards of backing fabric

80" square of quilt batting

Finished quilt: 74" square

Finished block: 15" square

Quantities specified are for 44/45"-wide 100% cotton fabrics. All measurements include ¼" seam allowances unless otherwise stated.

cut the fabrics

To make the best use of fabric, cut the pieces in the order listed. To make templates on the Pattern Sheet, follow instructions in Quilter's Primer, beginning on *page 179*.

This list includes the mathematically correct border lengths. For this project, strips are cut the length of the fabric (parallel to the selvage). You may add extra length to the strips now to allow for sewing differences later. Trim the border strips to the correct size before sewing them to the quilt top.

From muslin, cut:

- 2–4½×66½" border strips
- 2–4½×74½" border strips
- 288–2⅜" squares, cutting each in half diagonally for a total of 576 triangles, or 576 of Pattern A (page 54)
- 96–2" squares or 96 of Pattern B (page 54)
- 32–6³⁄₁₆" squares, cutting each in half diagonally for a total of 64 triangles, or 64 of Pattern D (Pattern Sheet)

From solid red, cut:

- 4–2×76" binding strips
- 2–3½×60½" border strips
- 2–3½×66½" border strips
- 352–2⅜" squares, cutting each in half diagonally for a total of 704 triangles, or 704 of Pattern A (page 54)
- 32–2" squares or 32 of Pattern B (page 54)
- 16–5" squares or 16 of Pattern C (Pattern Sheet)
- 32–5⅜" squares, cutting each in half diagonally for a total of 64 triangles, or 64 of Pattern E (Pattern Sheet)

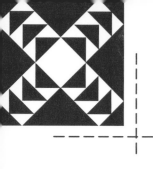

make the triangle-squares

To make a triangle-square, join one muslin A triangle and one solid red A triangle (see Diagram 1). Press the seam allowance toward the solid red triangle. Repeat to make a total of 576 triangle-squares (36 for each block). Each triangle-square should measure 2" square, including seam allowances.

Diagram 1
Make 576 triangle-squares

assemble the blocks

1. Referring to Diagram 2 for placement, lay out the pieces for one block. You'll need 36 triangle-squares, one solid red C square, six muslin B squares, two solid red B squares, four muslin D triangles, eight solid red A triangles, and four solid red E triangles.

here's a tip

Often too much time in an overly hot dryer shrinks cotton fabrics unnecessarily, as most shrinkage happens near the end of the drying cycle when the fabric is about 75 percent dry. If line-drying fabrics isn't an option, remove them from the dryer while damp and press them with a hot, dry iron.

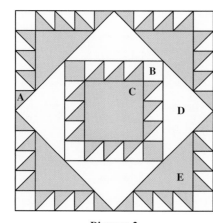

Diagram 2
King Solomon's Temple block

2. Sew together two rows of three triangle-squares (see Diagram 3). Press seam allowances toward one end. Join the units to each side of the solid red C square. Press seam allowances toward the solid red C square.

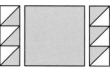

Diagram 3

3. Referring to Diagram 4, sew together two rows of three triangle-squares. Press seam allowances in one direction. Join a muslin B square and a solid red B square to the ends of each strip. Press seam allowances toward the squares. Sew one strip to the top of the solid red C square and one strip to the bottom. Press seam allowances toward the C square.

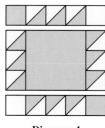

Diagram 4

4. Sew the long side of a muslin D triangle to one edge of the center unit. Join a muslin D triangle to the opposite edge (see Diagram 5, *opposite*). Press seam allowances toward the D triangles. Sew muslin D triangles to the remaining two sides; press seam allowances toward the D triangles. The center unit should now measure 11⅛" square, including seam allowances.

5. To make one outer corner unit, sew together three triangle-squares and one solid red triangle, as shown in Diagram 6, *opposite*. Press seam allowances in one direction. Sew the unit to the short side of a solid red E triangle. Press the seam allowance toward the E triangle.

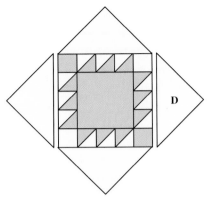

Diagram 5

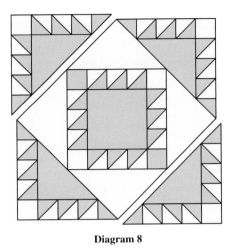

Diagram 8

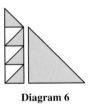

Diagram 6

Referring to Diagram 7, sew together three triangle-squares, one solid red A triangle, and one muslin B square. Press seam allowances toward the muslin square. Sew the unit to the remaining short side of the E triangle. Press the seam allowance toward the E triangle. Repeat to make four corner units.

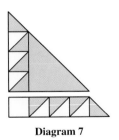

Diagram 7

6. Sew the long side of one corner unit to one edge of the center unit. Join another corner unit to the opposite edge (see Diagram 8). Press seam allowances toward the D triangles. Sew corner units to the remaining two sides. Press seam allowances toward the D triangles. The pieced block should

measure 15½" square, including the seam allowances.

7. Repeat Steps 1 through 6 for a total of 16 blocks.

assemble the quilt top

Lay out the 16 blocks in four rows of four blocks each. Sew together the blocks in each row. Press seam allowances in one direction, alternating the direction with each row. Join the rows.

assemble the borders

1. Sew one 3½×60½" solid red border strip to each side of the quilt top. Press seam allowances toward the border strips. Sew one 3½×66½" solid red border strip to the top of the quilt and one to the bottom. Press seam allowances toward the border strips.

2. For the outer border, sew one 4½×66½" muslin border strip to each side of the quilt top. Press seam allowances toward the border strips. Sew one 4½×74½" muslin border strip to the top of the quilt and one to the bottom. Press seam allowances toward the border strips.

complete the quilt

Layer the quilt top, batting, and backing according to instructions in Quilter's Primer, beginning on *page 179*. Referring to Diagram 9, outline-quilt or quilt in-the-ditch around each A and B piece and diagonally through the B pieces. Quilt diagonal cross-hatching ½" apart in pieces C, D, and E.

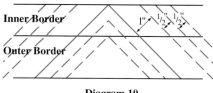

Diagram 10
Border Quilting Design

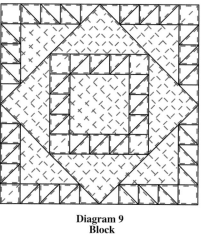

Diagram 9
Block
Quilting Design

To mark the design on the borders, draw parallel lines 1" apart at a 45-degree angle from the edge of the border (see Diagram 10). Mark a parallel line halfway between every previously drawn second and third line. Quilt on lines. If desired, the direction of the parallel lines may be reversed at the corners or center.

Bind the quilt according to the instructions in Quilter's Primer.

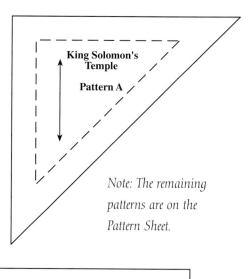

Note: The remaining patterns are on the Pattern Sheet.

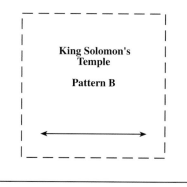

here's a tip

Adjust the tension on your sewing machine so it is balanced—allowing stitches on both sides of fabric to be free of loops, surface knots, and broken threads.

Make a Multicolor Version of this Two-Color Quilt

This dynamic pattern offers several design possibilities whether you use two fabrics or four; the results are stunning. Fabric combinations give the King Solomon's Temple block a contemporary, Southwestern, vintage, or floral twist.

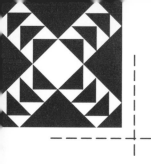

oregon trail quilt

Splashes of deep red twirl on this charismatic quilt, showcasing elaborate white-on-white quilting. The spritely corner motifs give unexpected zest at the borders.

materials

7¼ yards of white fabric
2½ yards of burgundy fabric
5¾ yards of backing fabric
90×108" precut quilt batting
Template material
Red embroidery floss (optional)

Finished quilt: 72×96"
Finished block: 12" square

designer notes

This quilt has an unusual set of 14 Oregon Trail blocks and 12 setting squares arranged around a plain center. This center area makes an ideal showcase for fancy quilting.

Finish the edges of the quilt by hemming the top and backing; then secure the edges with decorative embroidery. Apply a traditional binding if you prefer.

cut the fabrics

Refer to Quilter's Primer beginning on *page 179* for tips on making and using templates for patchwork. A window template is recommended for this block. Prepare templates for patterns A and B on *page 59.*

Before cutting, review the information on marking and cutting curves in the Quilter's Primer.

From white fabric, cut:

- 2–6½×86" borders
- 2–6½×62" borders
- 4–2¼×86" strips for straight-grain binding (optional)
- 1–36½" square
- 11–3½×42" strips. From these strips, cut 128 of Pattern A (page 59)
- 11–4×42" strips. From these strips, cut 112 of Pattern B (page 59)
- 12–12½" setting squares

From burgundy fabric, cut:

- 10–3½×42" strips. From these, cut 112 of Pattern A (page 59)
- 12–4×42" strips. From these, cut 128 of Pattern B (page 59)

assemble the blocks

1. Join white A pieces and burgundy B pieces along the curved edges to form squares. Make 128 square units in this coloration.

2. Make 112 square units in the opposite coloration, using burgundy A pieces and white B pieces.

3. Using two squares of each coloration, assemble four units into a quarter-block as show in Diagram 1, *page 58.* Make 56 quarter-blocks.

4. Referring to the assembly diagram, *page 58,* join four quarter-blocks into a complete block. Make 14 blocks.

5. Assemble the remaining 16 square units into four border corners as shown in Diagram 2, *page 58.*

oregon trail quilt continued

assemble the quilt top

1. Stitch pieced blocks onto opposite sides of one white setting square. Join this three-block row to one side of the 36½" center square. Repeat, joining another three-block row to the opposite side of the square.

2. Join the remaining blocks and setting squares in four rows of five blocks each. Two rows begin and end with pieced blocks, and two rows have setting squares at both ends. Press seam allowances toward the setting squares.

3. Join the rows and the assembled center section to complete the quilt top. Alternate the rows that begin with pieced blocks with those that begin with setting squares.

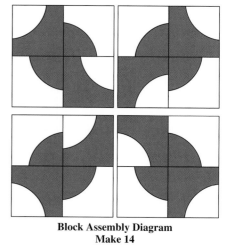

Block Assembly Diagram
Make 14

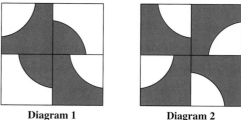

Diagram 1   Diagram 2

assemble the borders

1. Compare the 62"-long border strips with the top and bottom edges of the quilt. Trim the border strips so they are the same length as the edges. Stitch a border corner square to both ends of each strip.

2. Sew the 86"-long borders to the sides of the quilt top. Press the seam allowances toward the borders; trim excess border fabric.

3. Matching the corner seam lines with the side border seams, sew the pieced borders to the top and bottom edges of the quilt.

complete the quilt

Layer the quilt top, batting, and backing according to the instructions in Quilter's

Primer. Quilt as desired. The quilt shown has outline quilting around the seams of the patchwork.

To embroider the hem, trim the backing even with the quilt top. Trim the batting all the way around so it is ¼ inch smaller than the quilt top and back. Fold in a ¼-inch hem on both the quilt top and backing. Secure the folded edges with a decorative embroidery stitch.

If you prefer traditional binding, see the Quilter's Primer.

here's a tip

If you need to press a dark seam allowance toward a light piece, trim the sewn darker seam allowance slightly to prevent it from showing through.

Quilt Assembly Diagram

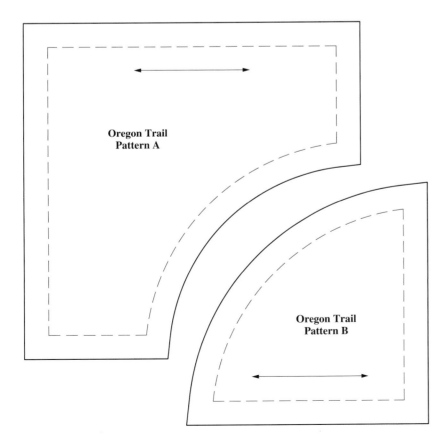

Oregon Trail
Pattern A

Oregon Trail
Pattern B

red bird quilt

Repetition of a single striking image, natural or abstract, often creates a quilt pattern with tremendous impact. As shown on this appliquéd quilt, the graceful silhouette of a bird in flight was a popular image among quilters of the late nineteenth century.

materials

4½ yards of muslin
2 yards of red fabric
4½ yards of backing fabric
Quilt batting
Black or navy embroidery floss
Water-erasable marker
Cardboard or plastic for templates

Finished quilt: approximately 70" square
Finished block: 14½" square

instructions

Enlarge the bird pattern, *below right*, and transfer to template material. Cut out. Block and border cutting measurements include ¼-inch seam allowances.

From muslin, cut:

- 2−6½×58½" borders
- 2−6½×70½" borders
- 16−15" squares
- 8½ yards of 2½"-wide bias binding

From red fabric, cut:

16 bird shapes, adding ¼" seam allowances

assemble the blocks

Mark an appliqué positioning guide on the blocks by tracing around the bird template pattern with a water-erasable marker. Position the bird shape on the background square with the beak slightly below the left middle of the block. Fold

here's a tip

At inside points for appliqué, make your stitches close together to prevent thread from raveling where you have clipped into the seam allowance. Secure an inside point with a single stitch.

under seam allowances around the bird; appliqué. Using either satin stitches or a large French knot, embroider eye. Make 16 blocks.

assemble the quilt top

1. Join the blocks into rows; make four rows with four blocks each. Stitch the rows together.
2. Stitch the shorter border strips to the top and bottom edges of the quilt top. Stitch remaining borders to the sides.

complete the quilt

1. To piece the quilt back, cut fabric into two 81-inch lengths. Cut or tear one length in half lengthwise. Sew one narrow panel to each side of the wide panel. Match the selvages; use a

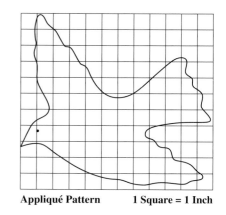

Appliqué Pattern   **1 Square = 1 Inch**

½–inch seam. Trim the seams to ¼ inch; press to one side.

2. Layer the back, batting, and the quilt top. Baste layers together; quilt as desired.

3. When quilting is complete trim away excess batting and backing so all edges are even with the quilt top. Fold the binding in half lengthwise, wrong sides together, and press. Sew the binding to the right side of the quilt, raw edges together. Turn the folded edge to the back; hand–stitch in place.

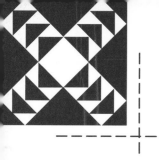

wild-goose chase

Stitching a quilt in just two colors provides dramatic results when there is a strong contrast between the two, as this red and white beauty illustrates. Black in combination with a bright color has the same result.

materials

5 yards of muslin for blocks, borders, and binding
4¼ yards of solid red for blocks and borders
5½ yards of backing fabric
84×100" of quilt batting

Finished quilt top: 75½×91"
Finished block: 12" square

Quantities specified are for 44/45"-wide 100% cotton fabrics. All measurements include a ¼" seam allowance unless otherwise stated.

cut the fabrics

To make the best use of your fabrics, cut the pieces in the order that follows. This listing includes the mathematically correct border strip lengths. For this project the strips are cut to the length of the fabric (parallel to the selvage). You may wish to add extra length to the strips now to allow for sewing differences later. Trim the border strips to the correct size before sewing them to the quilt top.

here's a tip
Mitered borders made of a print or striped fabric add complexity to the look of a quilt with little extra work. You may need to purchase extra fabric so all the corners will match.

From muslin, cut:
- *2–4×74½" border strips*
- *2–4×66" border strips*
- *31–4×12½" sashing strips*
- *9–2½×42" binding strips*
- *20–3⅞" squares for Position A*
- *240–2½" squares, cutting each in half diagonally for a total of 480 triangles for Position B (or cut 11–2½×42" strips into 480 triangles for Position B)*

- *24–2¾" squares, cutting each in half diagonally for a total of 48 triangles for Position G (or cut 2–2¾×42" strips into 48 triangles for Position G)*

From solid red, cut:
- *2–5½×81½" border strips*
- *2–5½×76" border strips*
- *12–3" squares for Position F*
- *20–8⅝" squares, cutting each diagonally twice in an X for a total of 80 triangles for Position D (or cut 5–8⅝×42" strips into 80 triangles for Position D)*
- *80–4⅝" squares, cutting each diagonally twice in an X for a total of 320 triangles for Position C (or cut 10–4⅝×42" strips into 320 triangles for Position C)*

assemble the rows

1. For one Flying Geese unit, use two muslin B triangles and one solid red C triangle.

2. Referring to Diagram 1, *below,* with right sides together, align diagonal edges of a muslin B triangle and the red triangle; sew together. Press the muslin triangle open. Then join the remaining muslin triangle to the opposite diagonal edge of the red triangle; press open. The pieced Flying Geese unit should measure

Diagram 1

wild-goose chase continued

2¼×3⅞", including the seam allowances (see Diagram 2).

3. Repeat Steps 1 and 2 to make a total of 240 Flying Geese units.

4. Referring to Diagram 3, join three Flying Geese units and one solid red C triangle to make a Flying Geese row. Repeat to make a total of 80 Flying Geese rows.

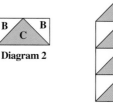

Diagram 2

Diagram 3

assemble the blocks

1. For one block you'll need one muslin A square, four Flying Geese rows, and four solid red D triangles.

2. Referring to the Block Assembly Diagram, *right*, lay out the pieces for one block as indicated. Sew together the pieces in sections. Join the sections. The pieced Wild-Goose Chase block should measure 12½" square, including the seam allowances.

3. Repeat Steps 1 and 2 to make a total of 20 Wild-Goose Chase blocks.

assemble the sashing corners

1. For one sashing corner you'll need one solid red F square and four muslin G triangles.

2. Referring to Diagram 4, sew a muslin triangle to opposite edges of the red square. Press the seam allowances toward the square. Join the remaining two muslin triangles to the raw edges

of the red square. Press the seam allowances toward the square. The sashing corner should measure 4" square, including the seam allowances.

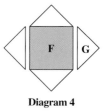

Diagram 4

3. Repeat Steps 1 and 2 to make a total of 12 sashing corners.

assemble the quilt top

Referring to the photograph, *opposite*, lay out four horizontal rows of five Wild-Goose Chase blocks and four muslin sashing strips each. Join the pieces in each row. Press the seam allowances toward the muslin sashing strips. Then lay out three horizontal rows of five muslin sashing strips and four sashing corners each. Sew together the pieces in each row. Press the seam allowances toward the muslin sashing strips.

Join the pieced rows, alternating block and sashing rows. Press the seam

here's a tip

To better see how a precut stencil's design will look when it's stitched, use a pencil to lightly trace through the stencil's cutout design onto tracing paper.

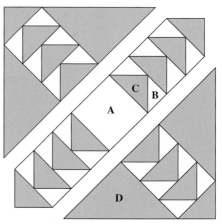

Block Assembly Diagram

allowances toward the sashing rows. The pieced quilt top should measure 59×74½", including seam allowances.

assemble the borders

1. Sew one 4×74½" muslin border strip to the top edge and to the bottom edge of the pieced quilt top. Press the seam allowances toward the muslin borders. Sew a 4×66" muslin border strip to each side edge of the quilt. Press the seam allowances toward the muslin borders.

2. Join a 5½×81½" solid red border strip to the top edge and to the bottom edge of the quilt top. Press the seam allowances toward the red borders. Sew one 5½×76" solid red border strip to each side edge of the quilt top. Press the seam allowances toward the red borders.

complete the quilt

Layer the quilt top, batting, and backing according to the instructions in Quilter's Primer beginning on *page 179*. Quilt as desired. Bind the quilt according to the instructions in Quilter's Primer.

here's a tip

A selvage is the tightly woven edge of a fabric bolt that runs along the lengthwise grain. It prevents each end of the bolt from raveling or fraying. A selvage is meant to be cut off and discarded. If you use a selvage, your finished quilt likely will have puckering and distortion.

sweet valentine quilt

Flowing quilted and appliquéd vines soften the look of this pieced quilt created in traditional Valentine's Day red and white. The corner doves bear hearts to express sweet sentiments.

 **pattern sheet**

materials

1¼ yards of red print No. 1 for blocks, sawtooth border, and outer border

1¼ yards of white print for blocks, sawtooth border, and bird, leaf, and vine appliqués

¼ yard of red print No. 2 for binding

⅞ yard of backing fabric

32×38" of quilt batting

Freezer paper (optional)

Finished quilt: 26×32"

Finished block: 6" square

Quantities specified are for 44/45"-wide 100% cotton fabrics. All measurements include a ¼" seam allowance. Sew with right sides together unless otherwise stated.

cut the fabrics

To make the best use of your fabrics, cut the pieces in the order that follows.

From red print No. 1, cut:
- 4–3½×26½" outer border strips
- 24–3" squares, cutting each in half diagonally for a total of 48 large triangles
- 90–1⅞" squares, cutting each in half diagonally for a total of 180 small triangles
- 4–1½" squares
- 48–1⅛×4¼" rectangles

From white print, cut:
- 24–3" squares, cutting each in half diagonally for a total of 48 large triangles
- 90–1⅞" squares, cutting each in half diagonally for a total of 180 small triangles
- 48–1⅛×4¼" rectangles

- 1–15" square, cutting it into two 1×15" bias strips for vine appliqués. For information on cutting bias strips, see the Quilter's Primer beginning on *page 179*.
- Appliqué bird and leaf shapes (Pattern Sheet)

From red print No. 2, cut:
- 4–2½×42" binding strips

assemble the blocks

1. With long edges aligned, chain-piece the 48 white print large triangles to the 48 red print 1⅛×4¼" rectangles (see Diagram 1). Cut the threads between each unit and press the seam allowances toward the white print triangles.

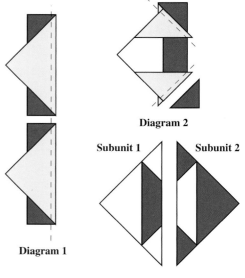

Diagram 2

Subunit 1   Subunit 2

Diagram 1

Diagram 3

2. Position two white print small triangles on a Step 1 Unit (see Diagram 2); sew together. Trim excess fabric from red print rectangle to complete a Subunit 1. Press seam allowances toward red print rectangle. Repeat to make a total of 48 of Subunit 1 (see Diagram 3).

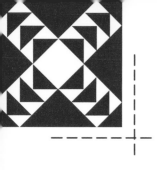

sweet valentine quilt continued

3. Repeat Steps 1 and 2 using the red print large and small triangles and the white print 1⅛×4¼" rectangles to make 48 total of Subunit 2 (see Diagram 3).

4. Sew together a Subunit 1 and a Subunit 2 to make a block. Press the seam allowance open. The pieced block unit should measure 3½" square, including the seam allowances. Repeat to make a total of 48 block units.

5. Referring to Diagram 4, lay out four block units in two rows. Sew together each row. Press the seam allowances in opposite directions. Sew together the rows to make a block. Press the seam allowance in one direction. The pieced block should measure 6½" square, including the seam allowances. Repeat to make a total of 12 blocks.

Diagram 4

assemble the quilt center

1. Lay out the 12 pieced blocks in four horizontal rows.

2. Sew together the blocks in each row. Press seam allowances in one direction, alternating the direction with each row. Join the rows to complete quilt center. Press seam allowances in one direction.

here's a tip

To avoid bearding, use black batting when quilting large areas of black fabric.

The pieced quilt center should measure 18½×24½", including seam allowances.

assemble and add borders

1. Sew together one white print small triangle and one red print small **Diagram 5** triangle to make a triangle-square (see Diagram 5). Press seam allowance toward red print triangle. The pieced triangle-square should measure 1½" square, including seam allowances. Make a total of 84 triangle-squares.

2. Sew together 24 triangle-squares to make a side sawtooth border strip. Press seam allowances in one direction. The pieced side sawtooth border strip should measure 1½×24½", including seam allowances. Repeat to make a second side sawtooth border strip. Add sawtooth border strips to side edges of pieced quilt center. Press seam allowances toward sawtooth border.

3. Sew together 18 triangle-squares to make the top sawtooth border strip. Press seam allowances in one direction. The pieced top sawtooth border strip should measure 1½×18½", including seam allowances. Repeat to make the bottom sawtooth border strip. Sew a red print 1½" square to each end of the top and bottom sawtooth border strips; press. Add the sawtooth border strips to the top and bottom edges of pieced quilt center. Press seam allowances toward sawtooth border.

4. Sew a red print 3½×26½" outer border strip to each side edge of pieced quilt center. Add the remaining red print

3½×26½" outer border strips to the top and bottom edges of the pieced quilt center to complete quilt top. Press seam allowances toward red print border.

prepare the vine appliqués

1. Fold a white print 1×15" bias strip in half lengthwise with the wrong side inside. Using a ⅛" seam allowance, sew the length of the strip (see Diagram 6).

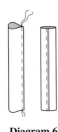

Diagram 6

2. Roll the strip so the seam is in the middle of one side; press flat to make a vine appliqué. Repeat to make a second vine appliqué.

prepare the appliqué pieces

Patterns are on Pattern Sheet. The following method uses freezer-paper templates.

From white print, cut:

- *2 each of patterns A and A reversed*
- *20 of Pattern B*

1. Lay the freezer paper, paper side up, over patterns A, A reversed, and B. Use a pencil to trace patterns A and A reversed each two times and Pattern B 20 times, leaving roughly ¼" between tracings; do not add any seam allowances or extensions. Cut out the pieces on the drawn lines, including the heart shape inside Pattern A, to make the freezer-paper templates.

2. Position the templates, shiny side down, on the wrong side of the white print fabric, leaving ¼" between templates.

3. Press the templates in place with a hot, dry iron. Lift the iron after five seconds

and check to be sure that each template has completely adhered to the fabric and that the fabric is not scorched.

4. Cut out each fabric shape, adding a ³⁄₁₆" seam allowance, to make the bird and leaf appliqués. Cut a scant ⅛" away from the freezer-paper edge of the heart shape. Clip the inside curves or points on the appliqué shapes where necessary; do not clip the outside curves.

appliqué the quilt top

1. Arrange the vine appliqués on the quilt top; baste. Appliqué the vines in place.

2. Arrange the leaf appliqués on the quilt top; baste. Appliqué the leaves in place, leaving a ½" opening along one edge of each. Using the opening for access, remove the templates by sliding your needle between the fabric and paper. Stitch the openings closed.

3. Arrange the bird appliqués on the quilt top; baste. Appliqué the birds in place, leaving a ½" opening along two opposite edges of each. Reverse-appliqué each center heart shape with small blind stitches, turning the edges under with your needle as you work. Remove the templates. Stitch openings closed.

complete the quilt

1. Layer the quilt top, batting, and backing according to the instructions in Quilter's Primer beginning on *page 179.*

2. Quilt as desired. The quilt on *page 65* has appliquéd vine and leaves pattern as the hand-quilting design in the side outer borders.

3. Use the red print 2½×42" strips to bind the quilt according to the instructions in Quilter's Primer.

here's a tip

If your batting is too small, you can join two batting pieces to make the necessary size. Follow this process to prevent a seam line ridge where the pieces join: overlap the batting pieces by several inches. rotary-cut a rolling curve through the overlapped area. Remove the excess and butt the curved edges together; use a herringbone stitch to join the two pieces.

Indigo and Prussian blues were popular quilting colors in the mid-1800s. These dark blue cotton and linen fabrics created a striking contrast against pure white to make this two-color combination a favorite throughout the years.

honeycomb & tree of life
In the late 1800s, quiltmakers frequently paired indigo and white fabrics in patterns that offered large open spaces to showcase their hand quilting. These two antique quilts exemplify the exquisite work done more than 100 years ago.

star chain quilt

Historic DaGama indigo print fabrics inspired this quilt that features contrasting stars. Indigo prints, originally produced in Central Europe, were introduced during the 1950s to South Africa, where they are currently printed.

materials

7 yards of cream print for blocks, setting squares, setting rectangles, and binding

20–18" squares of assorted indigo prints for blocks

5⅞ yards of backing fabric

74×104" of quilt batting

Finished quilt: 67½×97½"

Finished star block: 5" square

Quantities specified are for 44/45"-wide 100% cotton fabrics. All measurements include ¼" seam allowances unless otherwise stated.

select the fabrics

Although any indigo print fabric can be used to reproduce this quilt, there are some details to be aware of if you use DaGama indigos, which are printed using a 150-year-old process. Newly purchased fabrics are stiff. To soften the fabrics and remove excess dye, machine wash them several times in cold water with mild detergent. The fabrics also are printed on 36"-wide cloth rather than the traditional 44/45"-wide.

cut the fabrics

To make the best use of fabrics, cut the pieces in the order that follows.

From cream print, cut:

9–2½×42" binding strips

7–15½" setting squares

10–15½×10½" setting rectangles

58–5½" squares for Position E

264–1¾" squares for Position D

264–1¾×3" rectangles for Position A

130–2⅛" squares, cutting each in half diagonally for a total of 260 triangles for Position F

From assorted indigo prints, cut:

66–3" squares for Position C

528–1¾" squares for Position B (66 sets of 8 squares from the same fabric)

130–2⅛" squares, cutting each in half diagonally for a total of 260 triangles for Position F

assemble the star blocks

1. For one star block, you'll need four cream print D squares, four cream print A rectangles, and one set of matching indigo print pieces (one C square and eight B squares).

2. For accurate sewing lines, use a quilting pencil to mark a diagonal line on the wrong side of the indigo print B squares. (To prevent fabric from stretching as you draw lines, place 220-grit sandpaper beneath the squares.)

3. Right sides together, align a marked indigo print B square on one end of a cream print A rectangle (see Diagram 1 on *page 74*, noting placement of the marked diagonal line). Stitch on the marked line; trim the seam allowance to ¼". Press the attached triangle open.

4. Right sides together, align a second marked indigo print B square on the opposite end of the cream print A

here's a tip

If your sewing machine does not allow you to drop the feed dogs, tape a business card over them to prevent them from grabbing the fabric beneath the presser foot.

rectangle (see Diagram 1, noting placement of the marked diagonal line). Stitch on the marked line; trim and press to complete a Flying Geese unit. The pieced Flying Geese unit should measure 1¾×3", including seam allowance.

Diagram 1

5. Repeat Steps 3 and 4 to make a total of four Flying Geese units.

6. Referring to Diagram 2 for placement, lay out the four Flying Geese units and the remaining squares in three horizontal rows. Sew together the pieces in each row. Press seam allowances toward the squares. Join the rows to make a star block. Press seam allowances in one direction. The pieced star block should measure 5½" square, including the seam allowances.

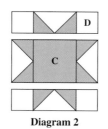

Diagram 2

7. Repeat Steps 1 through 6 to make a total of 66 star blocks.

assemble the units

Unit 1

1. For one Unit 1, you'll need five star blocks and four cream print E squares.

2. Referring to Diagram 3, lay out the squares in three horizontal rows. Sew together the squares in each row to make a Unit 1. Press seam allowances toward the cream print E squares. Join the rows. Press seam allowances in one direction. Pieced Unit 1 should measure 15½" square, including seam allowances.

3. Repeat Steps 1 and 2 to make a total of eight of Unit 1.

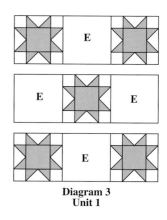

Diagram 3
Unit 1

Unit 2

1. For one Unit 2, you'll need three star blocks and three cream print E squares.

2. Referring to Diagram 4, lay out the squares in two horizontal rows. Sew together the squares in each row. Press seam allowances toward the cream print E squares. Join the rows to make a Unit 2. Press seam allowances in one direction. Pieced Unit 2 should measure 10½×15½", including seam allowances.

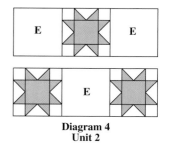

Diagram 4
Unit 2

here's a tip

When selecting a quilting pattern for a border, choose a design that fills the border's width well, keeping in mind you don't want the quilting to go too near the seam allowance or you'll risk covering it with the binding.

3. Repeat Steps 1 and 2 to make a total of six of Unit 2.

Unit 3

1. For one Unit 3, you'll need two star blocks and two cream print E squares.

2. Referring to Diagram 5, lay out the squares in two horizontal rows. Sew together the squares in each row. Press seam allowances toward the cream print E squares. Join the rows to make a Unit 3. Press the seam allowance in one direction. Pieced Unit 3 should measure 10½" square, including seam allowances.

3. Repeat Steps 1 and 2 to make a total of four of Unit 3.

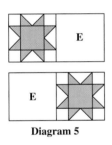

Diagram 5

assemble the quilt center

Referring to the photograph, *right*, for placement, lay out the 18 pieced units, the seven 15½" cream print setting squares, and the ten 15½×10½" cream print setting rectangles in seven horizontal rows. Sew together the pieces in each row. Press seam allowances toward the cream print setting squares or rectangles. Join the rows to complete the quilt center. Press the seam allowances in one direction. The pieced quilt center should measure 65½×95½", including the seam allowances.

assemble the borders

1. Sew together one indigo print F triangle and one cream print F triangle to make a triangle-square (see Diagram 6). Press the seam allowance toward the indigo print triangle. The pieced triangle-square should measure 1¾" square, including seam allowances. Repeat to make a total of 260 triangle-squares.

Diagram 6

2. Referring to the photograph, *below*, lay out 76 triangle-squares in a vertical row, noting placement of the triangle-squares. Sew together the triangle-squares to make a side border strip. Press seam allowances in one direction. Repeat to make a second side border strip. Join the side border strips to the side edges of the pieced quilt center.

3. Referring to the photograph, lay out 54 triangle-squares in a horizontal row, noting placement of the triangle-squares. Sew together the

triangle-squares to make the top border strip. Press seam allowances in one direction. Repeat to make the bottom border strip. Join the border strips to the top and bottom edges of the pieced quilt center to complete the quilt top.

complete the quilt

Layer the quilt top, batting, and backing following instructions in Quilter's Primer, *page 179*. Quilt as desired. The quilt shown is hand-quilted with an X in the stars and a feathered square design in the large blocks. A smaller feathered square design is quilted in the small blocks and a line is quilted in the border ¼" from the triangle points.

Use the 2½×42" cream print strips to bind the quilt following instructions in Quilter's Primer.

PILLOWCASE
materials

1¼ yards of cream print
8–9" squares of assorted indigo prints

Finished pillowcase: 27¾×42"
Finished star block: 5" square

Quantities specified are for 44/45"-wide 100% cotton fabrics. All measurements include a ¼" seam allowance unless otherwise stated.

cut the fabrics

To make the best use of your fabrics, cut the pieces in the order that follows.

From cream print, cut:
• *1–22×40½" rectangle*
• *1–6¾×40½" strip*
• *32–1¾" squares for Position D*
• *32–1¾×3" rectangles for Position A*
• *16–2⅛" squares, cutting each in half diagonally for a total of 32 triangles for Position F*

From assorted indigo prints, cut:
• *8–3" squares for Position C*
• *64–1¾" squares for Position B (this quilt features 8 squares from 8 different fabrics)*
• *16–2⅛" squares, cutting each in half diagonally for a total of 32 triangles for Position F*

assemble the pillowcase

1. Referring to Assemble the Star Blocks starting on *page 72*, make a total of eight star blocks.

2. Referring to the Pillowcase Assembly Diagram, sew together the eight star blocks in a vertical row. Press the seam allowances in one direction. Attach the 22×40½" cream print rectangle to the right-hand edge of star block row. Press seam allowance toward the star blocks.

3. Referring to Assemble the Borders, *page 75*, make a total of 32 triangle-squares.

4. Join the 32 triangle-squares in a vertical row. Press the seam allowances in one direction. Attach the 6¾×40½" cream print strip to the left-hand edge of the triangle-square row.

5. Join the triangle-square row to the left-hand edge of the star block row to make a 34½×40½" rectangle.

6. With right sides together, fold the 28¼×40½" rectangle in half. Sew raw edges together to complete the pillowcase; turn right side out.

7. Fold the long raw edge of the 6¾×40½" cream print strip under ½"; press. Fold the cream print strip to the wrong side of the pillowcase border; press. Machine-stitch in-the-ditch between the rectangle and the stars, catching the 6¾×40½" cream print strip in the stitching.

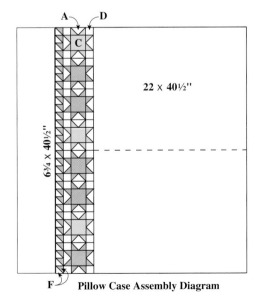

Pillow Case Assembly Diagram

A D

C

22 × 40½"

6¾ × 40½"

F

here's a tip
Match thread to fabric when you want the quilting design to blend in with the quilt top, such as when stippling or quilting in-the-ditch.

When you want to accentuate the quilting, choose a thread color to contrast the fabric.

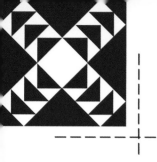

bow tie quilt

Enjoy a new technique for piecing the traditional Bow Tie block. Rotary-cut the fabrics; then machine-piece subunits to assemble into blocks without setting in seams. This makes it easy to create this cozy quilt.

materials

1¼ yards of blue and white plaid
   flannel No. 1 for blocks

1 yard of blue and white plaid
   flannel No. 2 for blocks

1 yard of blue and black plaid
   flannel No. 1 for blocks

3½ yards of solid navy flannel
   for blocks

⅜ yard of solid medium blue flannel
   for inner borders

2⅛ yards of blue and white plaid
   flannel No. 3 for outer borders

1¼ yards of blue and black plaid
   flannel No. 2 for binding

5 yards of backing fabric

71×87" of quilt batting

Finished quilt: 65×81"
Finished block: 8" square

Quantities specified are for 44/45"-wide 100% cotton flannels. All measurements include a ¼" seam allowance unless otherwise stated.

cut the fabrics

Because flannel shrinks, prewash and dry all fabrics twice.

To make the best use of your fabrics, cut the pieces in the order that follows. The outer border strips are cut the length of the fabric (parallel to the selvage). These measurements for the outer border strips are mathematically correct. You may wish to add extra length to the strips to allow for possible sewing differences.

From blue and white plaid flannel No. 1, cut:

• 6–4¾×42" strips
• 2–3×42" strips

From blue and white plaid flannel No. 2, cut:

• 7–2¾×42" strips
• 2–1¾×42" strips

From blue and black plaid flannel No. 1, cut:

• 7–2¾×42" strips
• 2–1¾×42" strips

From solid navy flannel, cut:

• 6–4¾×42" strips
• 14–2¾×42" strips
• 4–5½×42" strips
• 8–3¼×42" strips

From solid medium blue flannel, cut:

• 6–1½×42" strips for inner border

From blue and white plaid flannel No. 3, cut:

• 2–8×66½" outer border strips
• 2–8×65½" outer border strips

From blue and black plaid flannel No. 2, cut:

• 1–40" square, cutting it into enough 4½"-wide bias strips to total 310" in length for binding (for specific instructions, see Cut the Bias Strips, below)

cut the bias strips

Use a large acrylic triangle to square up the left edge of the 40" blue-and-black plaid flannel No. 2 block square and to draw lines at a 45° angle (see Bias Strip Diagram, *page 80*). Cut on the drawn lines

here's a tip

Have a project that calls for a specific size of square or rectangle? If the size is right, consider using a specialty triangle or square ruler instead of making a separate template.

bow tie quilt continued

to make bias strips. Handle the edges carefully to avoid distorting the bias. Cut enough strips to total the length needed.

Bias Strip Diagram

assemble the four-patch blocks

1. Align long raw edges of a 4¾×42" blue and white plaid flannel No. 1 strip and a 4¾×42" solid navy flannel strip; sew together to make a strip set (see Diagram 1). Press the seam allowance toward the blue and white plaid strip. Repeat for a total of six strip sets.

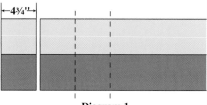

Diagram 1

2. Cut the strip sets into forty-eight 4¾"-wide segments.

3. Referring to Diagram 2 for placement, sew together two 4¾"-wide segments to make a large Four-Patch block. Clip the seam allowance just below the center intersection of the seams, cutting all the way to the stitching (see Diagram 3). Press the seam allowance as if it is two sections, pressing each one toward the plaid square (see Diagram 4). Repeat for a total of 24 large Four-Patch blocks.

Diagram 2

Diagram 3

Diagram 4

4. In the same manner as for the large Four-Patch blocks, make a total of seven strip sets using 2¾×42" blue and white plaid flannel No. 2 strips and 2¾×42" solid navy flannel strips. Cut the strip sets into ninety-six 2¾"-wide segments. Assemble the 2¾"-wide segments into 48 small Four-Patch blocks (see Diagram 5). Using the 2¾×42" blue-and-black plaid flannel No. 1 strips and the 2¾×42" solid navy flannel strips, make another 48 small Four-Patch blocks (see Diagram 5).

Diagram 5

In the same manner as for the large Four-Patch blocks, clip and press the seam allowances on all of the small Four-Patch blocks.

cut the four-patch blocks

1. Place a large Four-Patch block on a cutting mat so the outer corners of the two solid navy flannel squares are on a single vertical line (see Diagram 6, *opposite*). This line on the mat will be referred to as the corner line.

2. Place a ruler over the unit, aligning the 1" line on ruler directly on the corner line (see Diagram 7). Cut along the edge of the ruler using a rotary cutter.

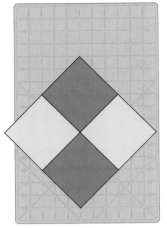

Diagram 6

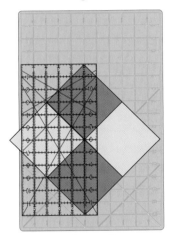

Diagram 7

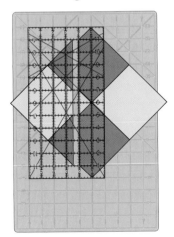

Diagram 8

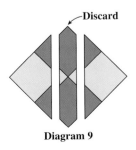

Diagram 9

3. Without moving the Four-Patch block, lift off the ruler, rotate the mat 180°, and set the ruler's 1" line directly on the corner line (see Diagram 8); cut. Discard the 2"-wide center section (see Diagram 9). Repeat with all large Four-Patch blocks to make 48 large triangles. The triangles do not need to remain in pairs.

4. Cut the small Four-Patch blocks into triangles in the same manner, except align the ruler's ⅜" line with the corner line. Discard the ¾"-wide sections. Make 96 small triangles from each fabric combination for a total of 192 triangles.

assemble the center units

1. Sew 5½×42" solid navy flannel strips to each long edge of two 3×42" blue and white plaid flannel No. 1 strips to make two strip sets (see Diagram 10). Press the seam allowances toward the plaid strips.

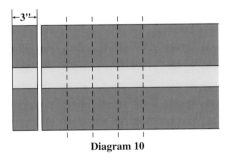

Diagram 10

2. Cut the strip sets into twenty-four 3"-wide segments for large center units.

3. Sew 3¼×42" solid navy flannel strips to each long edge of two 1¾×42" blue-and-white plaid flannel No. 2 strips to make two strip sets (see Diagram 11). Press the seams toward the plaid strips.

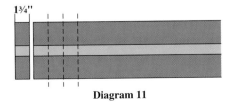

Diagram 11

here's a tip

Due to possible variances among manufacturers, it's preferable to use one brand of ruler throughout a project.

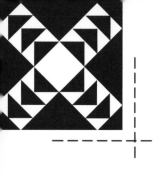

bow tie quilt continued

4. Cut the strip sets into forty-eight 1¾" wide segments for small blue and white center units.

5. Sew 3¼×42" solid navy flannel strips to each long edge of two 1¾×42" blue and black plaid flannel No. 1 strips to make two strip sets. Press the seam allowances toward the plaid strips.

6. Cut the strip sets into forty-eight 1¾"-wide segments for small blue and black center units.

assemble the bow tie blocks

1. For one large Bow Tie block, use two large triangles and one large center unit.

2. With raw edges aligned, center a large triangle over the center unit (see Diagram 12). Excess solid navy fabric remains at both ends. Sew the pieces together. Press the seam allowance toward the center unit.

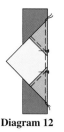

Diagram 12

3. Repeat Step 2 with the remaining large triangle on the opposite side of the large center unit to make a pieced large Bow Tie block.

4. Center and trim the pieced block to measure 8½" square, including the seam allowances.

5. Repeat Steps 1 through 4 for a total of 24 large Bow Tie blocks.

6. In the same manner, assemble 48 small blue and white Bow Tie blocks and 48 small blue and black Bow Tie blocks. Trim each pieced and trimmed small Bow Tie block to measure 4½" square, including the seam allowances.

assemble the quilt top

1. Lay out two small blue and white Bow Tie blocks and two small blue and black Bow Tie blocks in two horizontal rows of two blocks each (see Diagram 13). Sew together the blocks in each row. Press the seam allowances toward the blue and white blocks. Join the rows to make a four-block unit. The pieced four-block unit should measure 8½" square, including the seam allowances.

Diagram 13

2. Repeat with the remaining small Bow Tie blocks to make a total of 24 small four-block units.

3. Referring to the photograph, *opposite*, lay out the large Bow Tie blocks and the four-block units in eight horizontal rows, alternating blocks and units. Sew together the pieces in each row. Press the seam allowances toward the large Bow Tie blocks. Join the rows. The pieced quilt top should measure 48½×64½", including seam allowances.

assemble the borders

The following measurements for border strips are mathematically correct.

here's a tip

If your quilting is more than 1" from the outer edges, baste the layers together around the entire quilt ⅜" from the edges. This will prevent the outside of your quilt from ruffling and stretching as the binding is added.

Before cutting the border strips, measure your quilt top and adjust the lengths as necessary.

1. Cut and piece 1½×42" solid medium blue flannel strips to make the following:
- 2–1½×48½" inner border strips
- 2–1½×66½" inner border strips

2. Sew one medium 1½×48½" solid blue inner border strip to the top edge of the quilt top and one to the bottom edge. Join one medium 1½×66½" solid blue inner border strip to each side edge of the pieced quilt top. Press all seam allowances toward the inner borders.

3. Sew one 8×65½" blue-and-white plaid No. 3 outer border strip to the top and bottom of the pieced quilt top. Join one 8×66½" blue-and-white plaid No. 3 outer border strip to the side edges of the pieced quilt top. Press all seam allowances toward the outer border.

complete the quilt

Layer the quilt top, batting, and backing according to the instructions in the Quilter's Primer, beginning on *page 179*. Quilt as desired. Use the 4½"-wide blue-and-black plaid flannel No. 2 bias strips to bind the quilt according to the instructions in the Quilter's Primer.

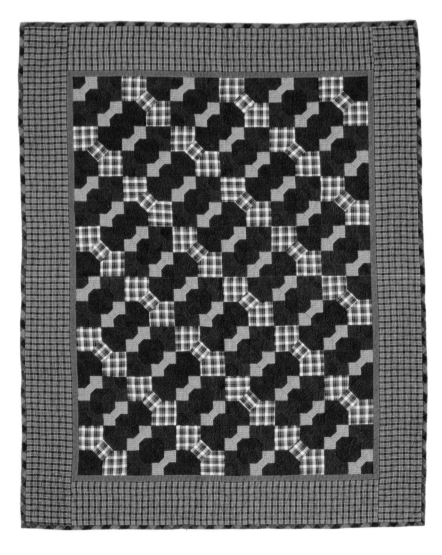

here's a tip

When pressing a long continuous binding strip in half, place two straight pins in your ironing surface with each shaft inserted to make an opening equal to half the width of the strip. Slide the end of the folded strip beneath the pins, then steadily pull the strip beneath the soleplate of a warm iron. The pins will fold the strip in half as it is pulled along. Note: Periodically lift the iron to prevent scorching the ironing board.

bluebirds flying

Bluebirds inspired the wall hanging, *opposite*, that captures their color. The project instructions guide your technique for setting in seams, reminding you how important it is to avoid sewing into the ¼" seam allowances.

materials

1½ yards of cream print for blocks, sashing, and borders

9–⅛–yard pieces of assorted medium or dark blue prints for blocks

1¼ yards of blue stripe for blocks and inner borders

1½ yards of medium blue print for outer borders and binding

2½ yards of backing fabric

55" square of quilt batting

Finished quilt: 49" square
Finished block: 10" square

Quantities specified are for 44/45"-wide 100% cotton fabrics. All measurements include a ¼" seam allowance unless otherwise stated.

cut the fabrics

To make the best use of your fabrics, cut the pieces in the order that follows. For this project, cut the border strips lengthwise (parallel to the selvage). This listing includes the mathematically correct border strip lengths. You may wish to add extra length to the strips now to allow for sewing differences later.

To make a template of the Diamond Pattern found on *page 87*, follow the instructions in the Quilter's Primer beginning on *page 179*. Transfer the dots marked on the pattern to the templates. The dots are the matching points.

here's a tip

With any marking tool, work with a sharp point to get a fine, yet visible line.

From cream print, cut:
- 2–2½×38½" sashing strips
- 4–2½×34½" sashing strips
- 6–2½×10½" sashing strips
- 18–3¼" squares, cutting each diagonally twice in an X for a total of 72 triangles
- 36–2½×4½" rectangles
- 36–2½" squares
- 4–2" squares

From each assorted medium or dark blue print, cut:
- 1–2½" square
- 2–2⅞" squares, cutting each in half diagonally for a total of 4 triangles
- 4 of Diamond Pattern (page 87)
- 4 of Diamond Pattern reversed (page 87)

From blue stripe, cut:
- 36 of Diamond Pattern (page 87)
- 36 of Diamond Pattern reversed (page 87)
- 4–2×38½" inner border strips

From medium blue print, cut:
- 5–2½×42" binding strips
- 2–4½×49½" outer border strips
- 2–4½×41½" outer border strips

assemble the blocks

When assembling the blocks for this quilt, set in seams. The key to setting angled pieces together is aligning marked matching points carefully. Whether you're stitching by machine or hand, start and stop sewing precisely at the matching points. This is an instance where it is necessary to backstitch to secure the ends of the seams. It prepares the angle for the next piece to be set in.

bluebirds flying continued

1. For one block use four 2½x4½" cream print rectangles, four 2½" cream print squares, eight cream print triangles, four blue stripe diamonds, four blue stripe reversed diamonds, and one set of medium or dark blue print pieces.

2. Pin together one blue stripe diamond and one medium or dark blue print reversed diamond (see Diagram 1). Carefully align the dots marked on the pattern. Sew together, making sure to avoid sewing into the ¼" seam allowances. Set in a cream print triangle (see Diagram 2). Repeat for a total of four diamond units. Then make a total of four mirror image diamond units with the remaining diamonds and triangles.

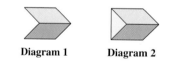

Diagram 1   **Diagram 2**

3. Sew together two diamond units, one of each kind (see Diagram 3), making sure to avoid sewing into the right angle's ¼" seam allowance. Then set in a cream print square as shown. Sew a medium or dark blue print triangle to the diamond units to complete the quarter unit. The pieced quarter unit should measure 4½" square, including the seam allowances. Repeat with the remaining diamond units, squares, and triangles for a total of four quarter units.

Diagram 3

4. Referring to Diagram 4 for placement, lay out the four quarter units, the cream print rectangles, and the medium or dark blue print square.

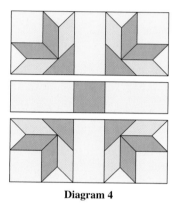

Diagram 4

5. Sew together the units in each row. Press the seam allowances toward the cream print rectangles. Join the rows. Press the seam allowances in one direction. The pieced block should measure 10½" square, including seam allowances.

6. Repeat Steps 1 through 5 for a total of nine blocks.

assemble the wall hanging

Referring to the photograph, *opposite*, for placement, lay out the nine pieced blocks and the 2½x10½" cream print sashing strips in three rows of three blocks each. Each row should begin and end with a block. Sew together the pieces in each row. Join the rows, alternating the rows with the 2½x34½" cream print sashing strips. Press the seam allowances toward the sashing strips. Then sew a cream print 2½x38½" sashing strip to each side edge of the joined rows. The pieced quilt center should measure 38½" square, including the seam allowances.

here's a tip

The fabric strength should be greater than that of the thread used for piecing. If seams are under stress, then the thread will give way before the fabric tears. For this reason, avoid strong polyester threads for piecing cotton fabrics.

assemble the borders

1. Sew one 2×38½" blue stripe inner
border strip to the top edge of the
pieced quilt center and one to the
bottom edge. Press the seam allowances
toward the blue stripe borders.

2. Sew a 2" cream print square to each
end of the remaining 2×38½" blue stripe
inner border strips. Join a pieced inner
border strip to each side edge of the
pieced quilt center. Press all seam
allowances toward the blue stripe border.

3. Sew one 4½×41½" medium blue print
outer border strip to each side edge of
the pieced quilt center. Join a 4½×49½"
medium blue print outer border strip to
the top edge of the pieced quilt center
and one to the bottom edge. Press all
seam allowances toward the dark
blue borders.

complete the wall hanging

Layer the quilt top, batting, and backing
according to the instructions in the
Quilter's Primer beginning on *page 179.*
Quilt as desired. Use the 2½×42" medium
blue print binding strips to bind the quilt
according to the instructions in
Quilter's Primer.

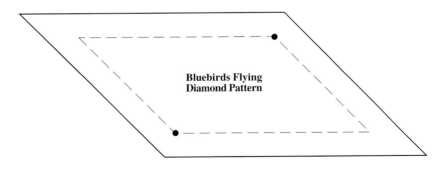

**Bluebirds Flying
Diamond Pattern**

settler's crossing

When Europeans crossed the Atlantic Ocean to explore North America, they likely used the stars as a navigational tool. The designers of this quilt had the stars in mind when they named this lap-size quilt that combines two different star blocks.

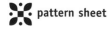 pattern sheet

materials

1¼ yards of navy print for blocks, setting squares, and borders

⅜ yard of dark teal print for Prairie Star blocks

½ yard of teal print for Prairie Star blocks

¾ yard of light teal print for Arrowhead blocks and Prairie Star blocks

5 yards of beige print for blocks, sashing, setting triangles, borders, and binding

3⅞" yards of backing fabric

69" square of quilt batting

Finished quilt: 63" square
Finished block: 7½" square

Quantities specified are for 44/45"-wide 100% cotton fabrics. All measurements include a ¼" seam allowance unless otherwise stated.

cut the fabrics

To make the best use of your fabrics, cut the pieces in the order that follows.

To make templates of the pattern pieces, found on the Pattern Sheet, follow the instructions in the Quilter's Primer, beginning on *page 179.*

From navy print, cut:

- *15–4¾" squares, cutting each diagonally twice in an X for a total of 60 triangles, or 60 of Pattern I*
- *4–4⅞" squares, cutting each diagonally twice in an X for a total of 16 sashing triangles*
- *32–3⅜" squares, cutting each in half diagonally for a total of 64 triangles, or 64 of Pattern H*
- *24–3" sashing squares*
- *12–2⅝" squares, cutting each in half diagonally for a total of 24 triangles, or 24 of Pattern J*
- *36–24⅜" squares, cutting each in half diagonally for a total of 72 triangles, or 72 of Pattern A*

From dark teal print, cut:
- *128 of Pattern D*

From teal print, cut:
- *128 of Pattern E*

From light teal print, cut:
- *128 of Pattern E*
- *45–2" squares or 45 of Pattern B*

From beige print, cut:
- *7–2½×42" binding strips*
- *3–12" squares, cutting each diagonally twice in an X for a total of 12 side sashing triangles*
- *2–6½" squares, cutting each in half diagonally for a total of 4 corner sashing triangles*
- *64–3×8" sashing rectangles*
- *36–2×3½" rectangles or 36 of Pattern C*
- *15–4¾" squares, cutting each diagonally twice in an X for a total of 60 triangles, or 60 of Pattern I*
- *32–3⅜" squares, cutting each in half diagonally for a total of 64 triangles, or 64 of Pattern H*
- *64–3¹⁄₁₆" squares, cutting each in half diagonally for a total of 128 triangles, or 128 of Pattern F*
- *12–2⅝" squares, cutting each in half diagonally for a total of 24 triangles, or 24 of Pattern J*

here's a tip

Is it hard to see the lines of your ruler on the fabric? When working with dark fabrics, choose a ruler with yellow or white markings. For light fabrics, choose one with black markings.

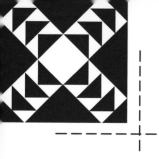

settler's crossing continued

- *64—2⁷⁄₁₆" squares, cutting each in half diagonally for a total of 128 triangles, or 128 of Pattern G*
- *36—2³⁄₈" squares, cutting each in half diagonally for a total of 72 triangles, or 72 of Pattern A*
- *36—2" squares or 36 of Pattern B*
- *128 of Pattern D*

assemble the arrowhead blocks

1. For one Arrowhead block use eight navy print A triangles, eight beige print A triangles, four beige print B squares, four beige print C rectangles, and five light teal print B squares.

2. Sew together one navy print A triangle and one beige print A triangle to make a triangle-square (see Diagram 1). Press the seam allowance toward the navy print triangle. The pieced triangle-square should measure 2" square, including the seam allowances. Repeat to make a total of eight triangle-squares.

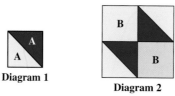

Diagram 1

Diagram 2

3. Referring to Diagram 2 for placement, lay out a beige print B square, a light teal print B square, and two triangle-squares in two rows. Sew together the squares in each row. Press the seam allowances toward the beige print and light teal print squares. Then join the rows to make a corner unit. Press the seam allowance in one direction. The pieced corner unit should measure 3½" square, including the seam allowances. Repeat to make a total of four corner units.

4. Referring to Diagram 3, lay out the four pieced corner units, four beige print C rectangles, and one light teal print B square in three horizontal rows. Sew together the pieces in each row. Press the seam allowances toward the beige print rectangles. Then join the rows to complete an Arrowhead block. Press the seam allowances in one direction. The pieced Arrowhead block should measure 8" square, including the seam allowances.

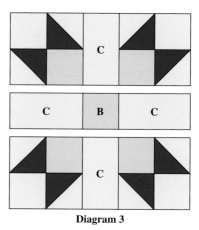

Diagram 3

5. Repeat Steps 1 through 4 to make a total of nine Arrowhead blocks.

assemble the prairie star blocks

1. For one Prairie Star block use eight beige print D triangles, eight dark teal print D triangles, eight teal print E pieces, eight light teal print E pieces, eight beige print G triangles, and eight beige print F triangles.

2. Referring to Diagram 4, sew together a beige print D triangle, a light teal print E piece, a teal print E piece, and a dark teal print D triangle to make a star point. Press the seam allowances in one direction. Repeat to make a total of eight star points.

Diagram 4

3. Referring to Diagram 5, sew a beige print G triangle and a beige print F triangle to a pieced star point to make a Subunit A. Press the seam allowances toward the beige print triangles. Repeat to make a total of four of Subunit A.

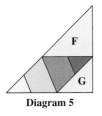

Diagram 5

4. Referring to Diagram 6, for a mirror image of Step 3, sew a beige print G triangle and a beige print F triangle to a pieced star point to make a Subunit B. Press the seam allowances toward the beige print triangles. Repeat to make a total of four of Subunit B.

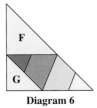

Diagram 6

5. Sew together a Subunit A and a Subunit B to make a quarter unit (see Diagram 7). Repeat for a total of four quarter units.

6. Referring to Diagram 8, lay out the quarter units in two rows. Sew together

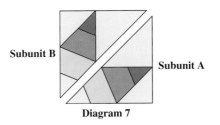

Diagram 7

the quarter units in each row. Press the seam allowances in one direction, alternating the direction with each row. Then join the rows to complete a Prairie Star block. Press the seam allowance in one direction. The pieced Prairie Star block should measure 8" square, including the seam allowances.

7. Repeat Steps 1 through 6 to make a total of 16 Prairie Star blocks.

assemble the quilt center

1. Referring to the Quilt Assembly Diagram, *page 93*, lay out the nine Arrowhead blocks, the 16 Prairie Star blocks, the 64 beige print sashing rectangles, the 12 beige print side sashing triangles, the 24 navy print sashing squares, and the 16 navy print sashing triangles in diagonal rows.

2. Sew together the pieces in each diagonal row. Press the seam allowances toward the beige print sashing rectangles. Then join the rows. Press the seam allowances in one direction. Join the four beige print corner sashing

Diagram 8

here's a tip

Before working on your project, do a test to see how the thread and needle combination works. Sew together long strips of fabric to test piecing or appliqué a patch. Create a little quilt sandwich (top, batting, and backing) and evaluate your quilting stitches.

triangles to complete the quilt center. Press the seam allowances toward the corner triangles.

Trim the beige print side and corner sashing triangles, leaving a ¼" seam allowance beyond the pieced block corners. The pieced quilt center should measure 56½" square, including the seam allowances.

assemble the border

1. Sew together one navy print H triangle and one beige print H triangle to make a triangle-square (see Diagram 1 on *page 90*). Press the seam allowances toward the navy print triangle. The pieced triangle-square should measure 3" square, including seam allowances.

2. Repeat Step 1 to make a total of 64 triangle-squares.

3. Referring to Diagram 9, *opposite*, lay out 16 triangle-squares, 15 navy print I triangles, and 15 beige print I triangles in diagonal rows. Sew together the pieces in each row. Press the seam allowances toward the navy print and beige print I triangles. Then join the rows to make a border row. Press the seam allowances in one direction. Attach a navy print J triangle and a beige print J triangle to each end of the pieced border row to complete a pieced border strip. Press the seam allowances toward the J triangles. The pieced border strip should measure 4×56½", including seam allowances.

4. Repeat Step 3 to make a total of four pieced border strips.

5. Sew a pieced border strip to the top and bottom edges of the pieced quilt

center. Press the seam allowances toward the pieced borders.

6. Sew together one navy print J triangle and one beige print J triangle to make a triangle-square. The pieced triangle square should measure 2¼" square, including the seam allowances.

7. Repeat Step 6 to make a total of 16 triangle-squares.

8. Referring to Diagram 10, *opposite*, lay out four triangle-squares in two rows. Sew together the triangle-squares in each row. Press the seam allowances in opposite directions. Then join the rows to complete a border corner block. The pieced border corner block should measure 4" square, including the seam allowances.

9. Repeat Step 8 to make a total of four border corner blocks.

10. Sew one corner block to each end of the remaining pieced border strips. Sew one pieced border unit to each side edge of the pieced quilt center to complete the quilt top. Press the seam allowances toward the pieced borders.

complete the quilt

Layer the quilt top, batting, and backing according to the instructions in the Quilter's Primer, beginning on *page 179*. Quilt as desired. The quilt on *page 89* is hand-quilted in-the-ditch. Using a 15"-diameter circle, the designer machine-quilted a simple arch in the sashing. Use the 2½×42" beige print strips to bind the quilt according to the instructions in the Quilter's Primer.

here's a tip
Typical thread weights are 30, 40, 50, 60, and 80. If the number of plies is equal, the higher number indicates finer thread. For example, a 50-weight three-ply thread is finer than a 40-weight three-ply thread.

Diagram 9

Diagram 10

Quilt Assembly Diagram

Make a Multicolor Version of This Two-Color Quilt

Use a bright, splashy batik print in the blocks and border for a focal point of a wallhanging using Settler's Crossing pattern. The blue squares and border keep the artsy look organized.

dutch blue

American cutwork designs such as this one find their roots in scherenschnitte, an elaborate form of paper cutting. To create the table mat, use freezer paper to cut out the design and transfer it to fabric.

 **pattern sheet**

materials

*¾ yard of indigo blue tone-on-tone
    print for cutwork appliqué
    and inner borders*
*¾ yard of light blue print for
    appliqué foundation and
    inner borders*
*⅞ yard of blue print for outer
    borders and binding*
1 yard of backing fabric
36" square of quilt batting
Freezer paper

Finished quilt: 32" square

*Quantities specified are for 44/45"-wide 100%
cotton fabrics. All measurements include a
¼" seam allowance unless otherwise stated.*

designer notes

Use small sharp scissors for snipping both paper and fabric; use a crafts knife on the freezer paper when trimming away the inside areas. Needle-turn appliqué and a very fine needle are recommended, such as a Sharp No. 10 or No. 11, to stitch the cutwork to the foundation.

cut the fabrics

To make the best use of your fabrics, cut the pieces in the order that follows. To make templates of the patterns found on *page 97*, follow the instructions in the Quilter's Primer, beginning on *page 179*.

From indigo blue tone-on-tone print, cut:

• *1–20" square for cutwork appliqué*
• *22–2⅞" squares, cutting each in half
    diagonally for a total of 44 triangles,
    or 44 of Triangle Pattern (page 97)*

From light blue print, cut:

• *1–22" square for appliqué foundation
    (trim to 20½" square after completing
    the appliqué)*
• *22–2⅞" squares, cutting each in half
    diagonally for a total of 44 triangles,
    or 44 of Triangle Pattern (page 97)*

From blue print, cut:

• *4–4½×32½" outer border strips*
• *4–2×42" binding strips*

From freezer paper, cut:

• *1–18" square*

appliqué the cutwork design

1. Fold the 18" freezer paper square in half horizontally, making a rectangle (see Diagram 1). Fold the rectangle in half, making a 9" square. Then fold the square in half diagonally, bringing together the folded edges. Staple the folds together in one corner to keep them stable.

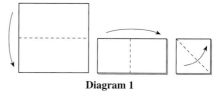

Diagram 1

2. Position the Heart Cutwork Pattern on the folded freezer paper as indicated.

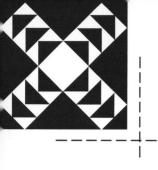

dutch blue continued

Tape or glue the pattern securely to the folded freezer paper. (If desired, use a dry-mount adhesive to allow the pattern to be removed and reused.)

3. Strategically pin or staple the layers to keep them from moving while cutting. Cut out the design carefully, including the inside open areas.

4. Carefully unfold freezer paper. Position the freezer paper shiny-side down on the 20" indigo blue tone-on-tone print square. Using a dry iron on cotton setting, press the freezer paper to the right side of the indigo fabric. Trace the outline of the cutwork design with a light-color fabric marker. These marks must remain visible throughout the appliqué process. Verify that every part of the design has been traced; then remove the freezer paper.

5. Match the center of the marked indigo blue square to the center of the 22" light blue print appliqué foundation square, aligning the straight edges. Baste through the center of the drawn heart cutwork pattern. The basting should hold the design in place until appliquéing is complete and should be out of the way of your needle-turn stitching.

6. Cut out the appliqué design a small portion at a time (about one-eighth to one-sixth of design), cutting a scant ⅛" away from the drawn lines so the lines can be your turn-under guide. Be careful to avoid cutting the foundation fabric. Snip deeply only inside the curves, and then sparingly. By cutting a little at one time, the piece remains more stable. Appliqué with small blind

stitches, turning the edges under with your needle as you work.

When appliquéing is complete, trim the light blue print foundation to measure 20½" square, including the seam allowances, centering the cutwork design.

assemble the inner borders

1. Sew together one indigo blue print triangle and one light blue print triangle to make a triangle-square (see Diagram 2). Press the seam allowance toward the indigo blue tone-on-tone print triangle. The pieced triangle-square should measure 2½" square, including the seam allowances. Repeat to make a total of 44 triangle-squares.

Diagram 2

2. Referring to the photograph, *page 95*, for placement, join 10 triangle-squares in a horizontal row to make the top inner border strip. Press the seam allowances in one direction. Repeat to make the bottom inner border strip. Sew the inner border strips to the top and bottom edges of the appliquéd quilt center. Press the seam allowances toward the appliquéd square.

3. Sew together 12 triangle-squares in a vertical row to make a side inner border strip. Press the seam allowances in one direction. Repeat to make a second side inner border strip. Sew the side inner border strips to the side edges of the

appliquéd square to complete the quilt center. Press the seam allowances toward the appliquéd square.

assemble the outer borders

1. With right sides together and midpoints aligned, pin a 4½x32½" blue print outer border strip to the top and bottom edges of the pieced quilt center and a 4½x32½" blue print outer border strip to each side edge; allow excess border fabric to extend beyond the edges. Sew each border strip to the quilt center, beginning and ending the seams ¼" from the corners (see Diagram 3). Press the seam allowances toward the border strips.

Diagram 3

2. To miter a border corner, overlap the border strips. Align the 90° angle of a right triangle with the raw edge of the border strip on top so the long edge of the triangle intersects the seam in the corner (see Diagram 4). With a pencil, draw along the edge of the triangle from the seam out to the raw edge. Place the bottom border strip on top and repeat the marking process.

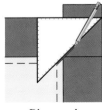

Diagram 4

3. With right sides together, match the marked lines and pin (see Diagram 5).

4. Beginning with a backstitch at the inside corner, stitch exactly on the marked lines to the raw edges of the border strips. Check the right side of the corner to see that it lies flat. Then trim the excess fabric, leaving a ¼" seam allowance. Press the seam open.

5. Miter the remaining corners in the same manner to complete the wall hanging top.

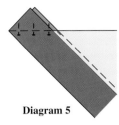

Diagram 5

complete the wall hanging

Layer the wall hanging top, batting, and backing according to the instructions in the Quilter's Primer, beginning on *page 179*. Quilt as desired. This quilt is hand-quilted around the appliquéd cutwork design, echoing the design with at least three lines spaced about ½" apart.

Use the 2x42" blue print strips to bind the quilt according to the instructions in the Quilter's Primer.

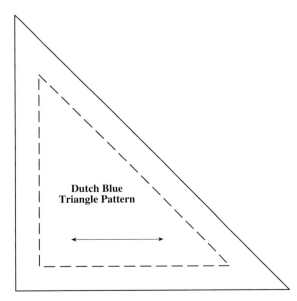

Dutch Blue Triangle Pattern

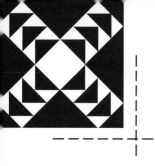

snow stars

Cool winter hues of blue and white give this bed-size quilt a clean, crisp finish. Whether you choose this color combination or a more dramatic grouping, such as the rendition on *page 103*, you're sure to find this project is easy to piece.

materials

2½ yards of dark blue print
    for blocks, borders, and binding
3¾ yards of light blue print for
    blocks and borders
2⅜ yards of white print for blocks
    and borders
4½ yards of backing fabric
79×94" of quilt batting

Finished quilt top: 72½×87½"
Finished block: 12½" square

Quantities specified are for 44/45"-wide 100% cotton fabrics. All measurements include a ¼" seam allowance unless otherwise stated.

cut the fabrics

The triangle pattern is on *page 103*. To make the best use of your fabrics, cut the pieces in the order that follows.

From dark blue print, cut:
- 8–2½×42" binding strips
- 14–1¾×42" strips for Four-Patch units
- 12–3" sashing squares
- 36–3×1¾" Position E rectangles
- 36–3×4¼" Position F rectangles
- 18–3×6¾" Position G rectangles
- 14–3×5½" Position H rectangles
- 28–3" Position C squares

From light blue print, cut:
- 80 Triangle Patterns (page 103)
- 31–3×13" sashing strips
- 7–1¾×42" strips for Four-Patch units
- 8–3×8" Position A rectangles

- 4–3×5½" Position B rectangles
- 188–3" Position C squares
- 14–1¾×3" Position D rectangles

From white print, cut:
- 28–1¾×42" strips for border and
    Four-Patch units
- 80 Triangle Patterns (page 103)

assemble the four-patch units

1. Aligning long raw edges, sew together one 1¾×42" dark blue print strip and one 1¾×42" white print strip to make a strip set. Press the seam allowance toward the dark blue strip. Repeat to make a total of 14 strip sets.

2. Referring to Diagram 1, cut a 1¾"-wide segment from a strip set. Repeat for a total of 320 segments.

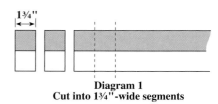

Diagram 1
Cut into 1¾"-wide segments

3. Sew together two 1¾"-wide segments to make a small Four-Patch unit (see Diagram 2, *page 100*). Press the seam allowance in one direction. The pieced small Four-Patch unit should measure 3" square, including the seam allowances. Repeat to make a total of 160 small Four-Patch units.

4. To make a large Four-Patch unit, use two small Four-Patch units and two light blue print C squares.

snow stars continued

Diagram 2
Make 160 small
Four-Patch units

Diagram 3
Make 80 large
Four-Patch units

Diagram 4
Make 80 triangle units

5. Referring to Diagram 3 for placement, lay out the Four-Patch units and squares in two rows. Sew together the squares in each row. Press the seam allowances toward the light blue print squares.

Join the rows. Press the seam allowance in one direction. The pieced large Four-Patch unit should measure 5½" square, including the seam allowances. Repeat to make a total of 80 large Four-Patch units.

assemble the triangle units

Referring to Diagram 4, join one light blue print triangle and one white print triangle. Press the seam allowance toward the light blue triangle. The pieced triangle unit should measure 3×5½", including the seam allowances. Repeat to make a total of 80 triangle units.

assemble the blocks

1. For one block use four large Four-Patch units, four triangle units, and one light blue C square.

2. Referring to Diagram 5 for placement, lay out the units and the square in three horizontal rows. Sew together the pieces in each row. Press the seam allowances toward the triangle units; join the rows. The pieced block should measure 13" square, including the seam allowances.

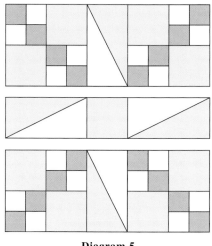

Diagram 5
Make 20 blocks

3. Repeat Steps 1 and 2 to make a total of 20 blocks.

assemble the quilt top

Referring to the photograph, *opposite*, for placement, lay out the blocks, sashing strips, and sashing squares in horizontal rows. Sew together the pieces in each row. Press the seam allowances toward the sashing strips. Then join the rows. Press the seam allowances in one direction. The pieced quilt top should measure 58×73", including the seam allowances.

assemble the borders

1. Cut and piece seven 1¾×42" white print strips to make the following:
- 2–1¾×58" border strips
- 2–1¾×73" border strips

2. Aligning long raw edges, sew together one 1¾×42" white print strip and one 1¾×42" light blue print strip to

here's a tip

If you want to select another hue in a quilt but don't want to add another color, select brown. It provides contrast and transition.

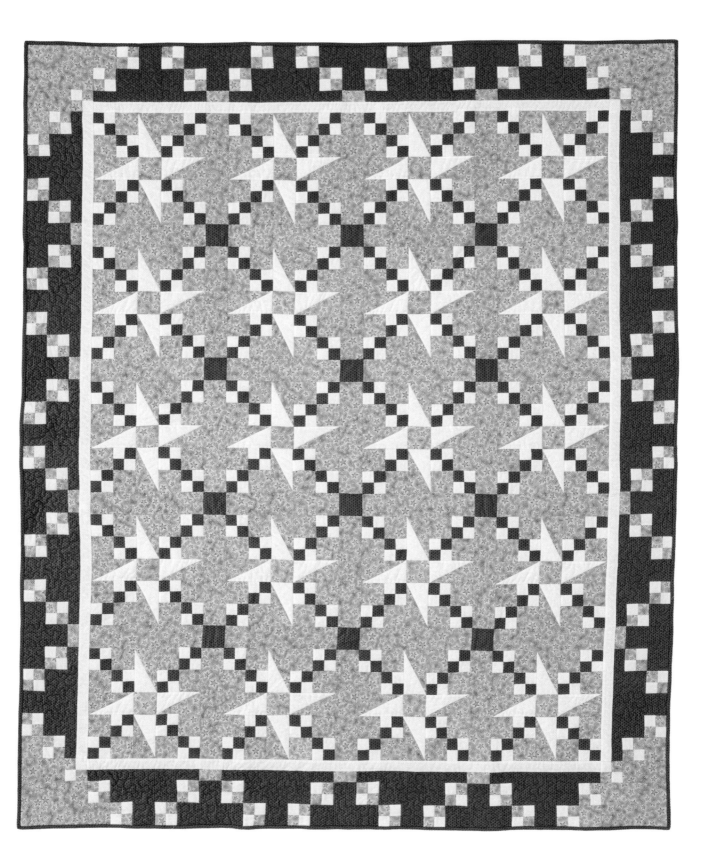

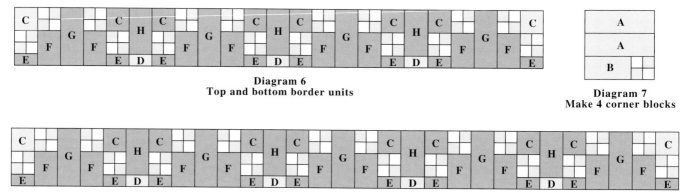

Diagram 6
Top and bottom border units

Diagram 7
Make 4 corner blocks

Diagram 8
Side border units

make a strip set. Press the seam allowance toward the light blue strip. Repeat for a total of seven strip sets.

3. Cut a 1¾"-wide segment from a strip set. Repeat for a total of 152 segments. Combine two segments into a small Four-Patch unit in the same manner as before. Repeat to make a total of 76 light blue and white small Four-Patch units.

4. For a top border unit use 16 light blue and- white small Four-Patch units, six dark blue print C squares, two light blue print C squares, three light blue print D rectangles, eight dark blue print E rectangles, eight dark blue print F rectangles, four dark blue print G rectangles, and three dark blue print H rectangles.

5. Referring to Diagram 6, lay out the pieces for the top border unit. Sew together the pieces in vertical sections. Then join the sections. The pieced top border unit should measure 6¾×58", including the seam allowances.

here's a tip

To plan your own quilt blocks, use colored pencils and graph paper to record the design.

6. Sew one white 1¾×58" print border strip to the bottom edge of the top border unit. Join the border unit to the top edge of the pieced quilt top.

7. Repeat Steps 3 through 6 for the bottom border unit. Join the border unit to the bottom edge of the pieced quilt top.

8. For a corner block use one light blue and white small Four-Patch unit, one light blue print B rectangle, and two light blue print A rectangles.

9. Referring to Diagram 7 for placement, lay out the pieces as shown. Sew together the B rectangle and the small Four-Patch unit. Press the seam allowance toward the B rectangle. Then join the rows. Press the seam allowances in one direction. The pieced corner block should measure 8" square, including the seam allowances.

10. Repeat Steps 8 and 9 to make a total of four corner blocks.

11. For a side border unit use 20 light blue and white small Four-Patch units, eight dark blue print C squares, two light blue print C squares, four light blue print D rectangles, 10 dark blue print E rectangles, 10 dark blue print F rectangles, five dark blue print G rectangles, and four dark blue print H rectangles.

12. Referring to Diagram 8, lay out the pieces for a side border unit. Sew together the pieces in vertical sections. Then join the sections. The pieced side border unit should measure 6¾×73", including the seam allowances.

13. Sew one 1¾×73" white print border strip to the bottom edge of the side border unit. Join a corner block to each end of the side border unit. Join the border unit to one side edge of the pieced quilt top.

14. Repeat Steps 11 through 13 for a second side border unit. Join the border unit to the remaining side edge of the pieced quilt top.

complete the quilt

Layer the quilt top, batting, and backing according to the instructions in the Quilter's Primer beginning on *page 179*. Quilt as desired. Bind according to the instructions in the Quilter's Primer.

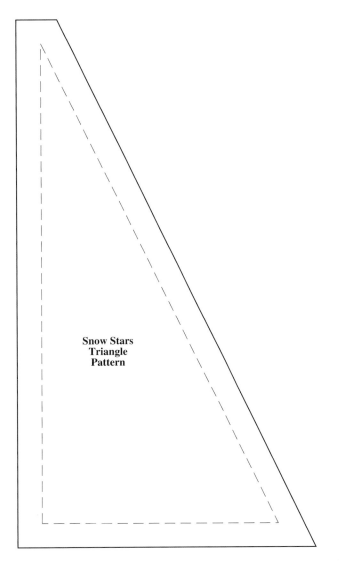

Snow Stars
Triangle
Pattern

Make a Multicolor Version of This Two-Color Quilt

Create a darker coloration of this pattern with a black background and star and moon motifs in purple, turquoise, and orange. Choose additional prints to finish the pattern.

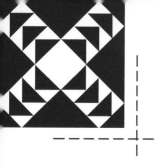

blue and white

Several shades of blue combine with pure white on this lively quilt. The two-color blocks are placed to alternate background colors, lending an abstract checkered design that is full of movement.

materials

1½ yards of solid white for blocks

7–½-yard pieces of solid blue in shades ranging from light to dark for blocks, borders, and binding

3 yards of backing fabric

54×66" of quilt batting

Finished quilt top: 48×60"

Finished block: 6" square

Quantities specified are for 44/45"-wide 100% cotton fabrics. All measurements include a ¼" seam allowance unless otherwise stated.

cut the fabrics

To make the best use of your fabrics, cut the pieces in the order that follows. The Triangle Pattern can be found on *page 107*. To make a template of the pattern, follow the instructions in the Quilter's Primer beginning on *page 179*.

Before cutting any fabrics, set aside the lightest blue fabric for binding. From the six remaining blue fabrics, separate out the darkest blue and cut enough pieces to make 13 blocks (seven with blue stars and six with white stars). Finally, cut enough pieces from the remaining five blue fabrics to make 10 blocks each (five with blue stars and five with white stars from each blue fabric).

blue and white continued

From solid white, cut:
- *124–2×3½" rectangles*
- *252 of Triangle Pattern (page107)*

From each of five solid blues, cut:
- *20–2×3½" rectangles*
- *52 of Triangle Pattern (page107)*

assemble the blocks

1. For one blue star block use four blue triangles of the same fabric, four white triangles, and four 2×3½" white rectangles.

2. Sew together a blue triangle and a white triangle to make a blue star point (see Diagram 1). Press the seam allowance toward the blue triangle. The pieced star point should measure 2×3½", including the seam allowances. Repeat to make a total of four blue star points.

Diagram 1

3. Sew a 2×3½" white rectangle to the long white edge of each blue star point to make four blue star point units (see Diagram 2).

Diagram 2

4. Referring to Diagram 3, *below*, for placement, lay out the four blue star point units in two horizontal rows.

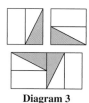

Diagram 3

Sew together the units in each row. Press the seam allowances in opposite directions. Then join the rows to make a star block. Press the seam allowance open. The pieced blue star block should measure 6½" square, including the seam allowances.

5. Repeat Steps 1 through 4 to make a total of 31 blue star blocks.

6. For one white star block use four blue triangles and four 2×3½" blue rectangles of the same fabric and four white triangles.

7. Repeat Step 2 to make a total of four white star points. Sew a 2×3½" blue rectangle to the long blue edge of each white star point to make four white star point units (see Diagram 4).

Diagram 4

8. Repeat Step 4 using the four white star point units to piece a white star block (see Diagram 5).

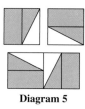

Diagram 5

9. Repeat Steps 6 through 8 to make a total of 32 white star blocks.

assemble the quilt center

Referring to the photograph, *page 105,* lay out the blue star blocks and the white star blocks in nine horizontal rows. When you're pleased with the arrangement, sew

here's a tip

To take quilting with you when traveling, lay pieces of a block on batting and carefully roll them up inside.

together the blocks in each row. Press the seam allowances in one direction, alternating the direction for each row. Then join the rows to complete the quilt center. The pieced quilt center should measure 42½×54½", including the seam allowances.

assemble the borders

From solid medium–light blue, cut:
- *1–3½×42½" border strip*

From solid blue, cut:
- *1–3½×42½" border strip*

From solid medium–dark blue, cut:
- *2–3½×42" border strips*

From solid dark blue, cut:
- *2–3½×42" border strips*

From solid darkest blue, cut:
- *4–3½" squares*

1. Sew a solid medium-light blue 3½×42½" border strip to the top edge and a solid blue 3½×42½" border strip to the bottom edge of the pieced quilt center. Press the seam allowances toward the blue border.

2. Piece the solid medium-dark blue 3½×42" border strips to make the following:
- *1–3½×54½" border strip*

3. Piece the solid dark blue 3½×42" border strips to make the following:
- *1–3½×54½" border strip*

4. Sew a solid darkest blue 3½" square to each end of the solid medium-dark blue 3½×54½" border strip and the solid dark blue 3½×54½" border strip to make two pieced border units. Sew a pieced border unit to each side edge of the pieced quilt center to complete the quilt top. Press the seam allowances toward the blue border.

complete the quilt

From lightest solid blue, cut:
- *6–2½×42" binding strips*

Layer the quilt top, batting, and backing according to the instructions in the Quilter's Primer beginning on *page 179*. Quilt as desired. This quilt used concentric circles for the quilting design. Use the lightest solid blue 2½×42" strips to bind the quilt according to the instructions in the Quilter's Primer.

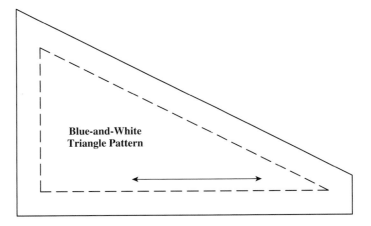

Blue-and-White Triangle Pattern

honeycomb and tree of life quilts

Both of these antique quilts combine indigo and white fabrics in patterns that leave large open spaces to showcase hand quilting. For a closer look at the patterns, see *page 110* for the honeycomb design and *page 112* for the tree of life.

materials for the honeycomb

4½ yards of muslin for blocks and border
2⅓ yards of blue print for blocks and binding
4 yards of backing fabric
71×80" of quilt batting

Finished quilt: 65×74"
Finished block: 9" square

Quantities specified are for 44/45"-wide 100% cotton fabrics. All measurements include a ¼" seam allowance unless otherwise stated.

cut the fabrics

To make the best use of your fabrics, cut the pieces in the order that follows. Cut all strips across the width of the fabric. As you cut pieces for the various strip sets, label them and put them aside in sets to avoid confusion later.

From muslin, cut:
- 28–5½×9½" *rectangles for Alternate blocks*
- 56–2½×5½" *rectangles for Alternate blocks*
- 112–3½" *squares for Nine-Patch blocks*
- 36–1½×42" *strips for blocks and border*

From blue print, cut:
- 33–1½×42" *strips for blocks*
- 7–2½×42" *binding strips*

assemble the nine-patch blocks

1. Aligning long edges, sew two 1½×42" blue print strips to a 1½×42" muslin strip to make a Strip Set A (see Diagram 1).

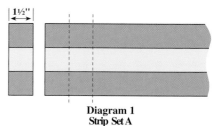

Diagram 1
Strip Set A

Press the seam allowances toward the blue print strips. Repeat to make a total of 10 of Strip Set A. Cut the Strip Sets into 1½"-wide segments to total 280.

2. Aligning long edges, sew two 1½×42" muslin strips to a 1½×42" blue print strip to make a Strip Set B (see Diagram 2). Press the seam allowances toward the blue print strip. Repeat to make a total of five of Strip Set B. Cut the Strip Sets into 1½"-wide segments for a total of 140.

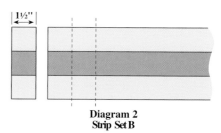

Diagram 2
Strip Set B

3. Sew together two Strip Set A segments and one Strip Set B segment to make a Nine-Patch unit (see Diagram 3). Press the seam allowances toward the center segment. The Nine-Patch unit should measure 3½" square, including the seam

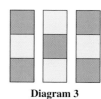

Diagram 3

honeycomb continued

allowances. Repeat to make a total of 140 Nine-Patch units.

4. Referring to Diagram 4 for placement, lay out five Nine-Patch units and four 3½" muslin squares in three horizontal rows. Sew together the pieces in each row. Press the seam allowances toward

the muslin squares. Then join the rows to make a Nine-Patch block. Press the seam allowances in one direction. The pieced Nine-Patch block should measure 9½" square, including the seam allowances.

5. Repeat Step 4 to make a total of 28 Nine-Patch blocks.

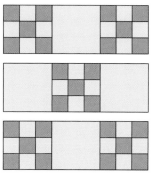

Diagram 4

assemble the alternate blocks

1. Aligning long edges, sew together one 1½×42" muslin strip and one 1½×42" blue print strip to make a Strip Set C (see Diagram 5). Press the seam allowance toward the blue print strip. Repeat to make a total of eight of Strip Set C. Cut the Strip Sets into 1½"-wide segments for a total of 224.

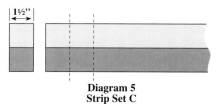

Diagram 5
Strip Set C

2. Lay out two Strip Set C segments as shown in Diagram 6. Sew together to make a Four-Patch block. Press the seam allowance in one direction. The pieced Four-Patch block should measure 2½" square, including the seam allowances. Repeat to make a total of 112 Four-Patch blocks.

Diagram 6

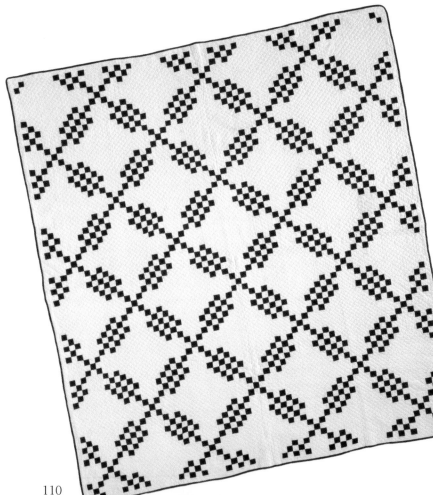

3. Referring to Diagram 7, lay out four Four-Patch blocks, two 2½x5½" muslin rectangles, and one 5½x9½" muslin rectangle in three horizontal rows.

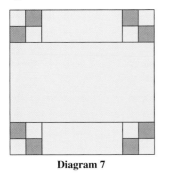

Diagram 7

Sew together the pieces in each row. Press the seam allowances toward the muslin rectangles. Then join the rows to make an Alternate block. Press the seam allowances in one direction. The pieced Alternate block should measure 9½", including the seam allowances.

4. Repeat Step 3 to make a total of 28 Alternate blocks.

assemble the quilt center

Referring to the photograph, *opposite*, lay out the Nine-Patch blocks and Alternate blocks in eight horizontal rows. Sew together the blocks in each row. Press the seam allowances toward the Alternate blocks. Then join the rows to complete the quilt center. Press the seam allowances in one direction. The pieced quilt center should measure 63½x72½", including the seam allowances.

assemble the border

These measurements for border strips are mathematically correct. Before cutting the strips, measure your pieced quilt center and adjust the lengths as necessary.

1. Cut and piece the remaining 1½x42" muslin strips to measure as follows:
  • 2–1½x74½" border strips
  • 2–1½x63½" border strips

2. Sew one 1½x63½" muslin border strip to the top and bottom edges of the pieced quilt center. Then join a 1½x74½" muslin border strip to each side edge of the quilt center to complete the quilt top. Press all seam allowances toward the muslin borders.

complete the quilt

Layer the quilt top, batting, and backing according to the instructions in the Quilter's Primer beginning on *page 179*. Quilt as desired. Use the 2½x42" blue print strips to bind the quilt according to the instructions in the Quilter's Primer.

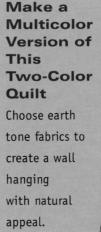

Make a Multicolor Version of This Two-Color Quilt

Choose earth tone fabrics to create a wall hanging with natural appeal.

tree of life quilt

 **pattern sheet**

materials for the tree of life

*4½ yards of muslin for blocks, setting squares,
and setting and corner triangles*

2 yards of blue print for blocks

⅝ yard of solid blue for binding

3⅛ yards of backing fabric

56×82" of quilt batting

Finished quilt: 51×76½"

Finished block: 9" square

*Quantities specified are for 44/45"-wide 100%
cotton fabrics. All measurements include a
¼" seam allowance unless otherwise stated.*

cut the fabrics

To make the best use of your fabrics, cut
the pieces in the order that follows.

The patterns are on the Pattern Sheet.
To make templates from the pattern pieces,
follow the instructions in Quilter's Primer,
beginning on *page 179*.

The setting and corner triangles are cut
slightly larger than necessary. Trim them to
the correct size after piecing the quilt top.

From muslin, cut:

- *4–15" squares, cutting each diagonally twice
  in an X for a total of 16 setting triangles*
- *15–9½" squares for setting squares*
- *2–9" squares, cutting each in half diagonally
  for a total of four corner triangles*
- *48–2×4" rectangles or 48 of Pattern I*
- *24 each of patterns E and E reversed*
- *24–3⅞" squares, cutting each in half
  diagonally for a total of 48 triangles or 48 of
  Pattern C*
- *12–3⅜" squares, cutting each in half
  diagonally for a total of 24 triangles or 24 of
  Pattern G*
- *360–1⅞" squares, cutting each in half
  diagonally for a total of 720 triangles or 720
  of Pattern A*
- *72–1½" squares or 72 of Pattern B*

From blue print, cut:

- *12–4⅞" squares, cutting each in half
  diagonally for a total of 24 triangles or 24 of
  Pattern D*
- *24–1⅞×3⅜" rectangles or 24 of Pattern F*
- *24 of Pattern H*
- *432–1⅞" squares, cutting each in half
  diagonally for a total of 864 triangles
  or 864 of Pattern A*

From solid blue, cut:

- *7–2½×42" binding strips*

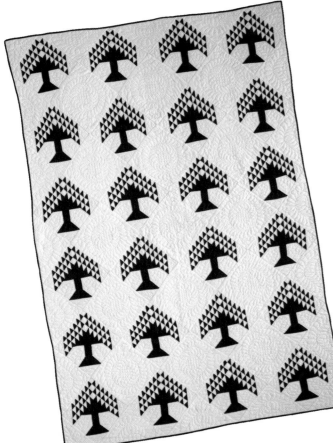

assemble the blocks

1. For one Tree of Life block, use 30 muslin A triangles, 36 blue print A triangles, three muslin B squares, two muslin C triangles, one blue print D triangle, one muslin E piece, one muslin E reversed piece, one blue print F rectangle, one muslin G triangle, one blue print H piece, and two muslin I rectangles.

2. Sew together one muslin A triangle and one blue print A triangle to make a triangle-square (see Diagram 1). Press the seam allowance toward the blue print triangle. The pieced triangle-square should measure 1½" square, including the seam allowances. Repeat to make a total of 30 triangle-squares (six blue print A triangles remain unused at this point).

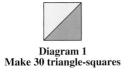

Diagram 1
Make 30 triangle-squares

3. Referring to Diagram 2 for placement, sew together the triangle-squares, the remaining six blue print A triangles, and the muslin B squares in two sections. Join a muslin C triangle to the diagonal end of each section.

4. Join the muslin E piece and the muslin E reversed piece to the long edges of the blue print F rectangle. Avoid sewing into the seam allowances in the angled corners. Press the seam allowances toward the blue print rectangle.

5. Sew the blue print D triangle to the straight edge of the E/F/E unit.

6. Sew the muslin I rectangles to the D/E/F/E unit. Avoid sewing into the seam allowances in the angled corners. Press the seam allowances toward the muslin rectangles.

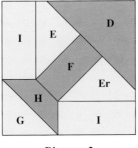

Diagram 2

7. Sew a muslin G triangle to a blue print H piece. Set G/H unit into D/E/F/E/I/I unit to complete third section.

8. Join the three sections to complete a Tree of Life block. The pieced block should measure 9½" square, including the seam allowances.

9. Repeat Steps 1 through 8 to make a total of 24 Tree of Life blocks.

assemble the quilt top

1. Referring to the photograph, *opposite,* lay out the 24 blocks, the 15 setting squares, and the 16 setting triangles in diagonal rows. Sew together the pieces in each row. Press seam allowances in one direction, alternating each row. Join the rows to complete the quilt center. Press seam allowances in one direction.

2. Join the muslin corner triangles to the quilt top. Press the seam allowances toward the corner triangles.

3. Trim the quilt top, leaving a ¼" seam allowance beyond the block corners. The pieced quilt top should measure 51½x77", including seam allowances.

complete the quilt

Layer quilt top, batting, and backing according to the instructions in Quilter's Primer, beginning on *page 179.* Quilt as desired. Use the 2½x42" solid blue strips to bind the quilt as in Quilter's Primer.

here's a tip
The arrow symbol (◄─►) represents the direction the grain line should run when fabric pieces are cut.

kalona star quilt

Eight-point blue stars nestle inside larger white stars to form a heavenly pattern. This charming blue and white quilt is edged with interlocking prairie points, creating a variegated zigzag edge.

materials

9 yards of cream fabric

5 yards each of light blue and medium blue print fabric

4 yards of medium blue print fabric

9 yards of backing fabric

Quilt batting

Cardboard or plastic for templates

Finished quilt: 94×114"

Finished block: 20" square

Quantities specified are for 44/45"-wide 100% cotton fabrics. All patterns are finished size; add ¼" seam allowances when cutting the pieces from fabric unless otherwise stated.

cut the fabrics

To make the best use of your fabrics, cut the pieces in the order that follows. Pattern A is on *page 117*. To make a template of the pattern, follow the instruction in the Quilter's Primer beginning on *page 179*.

For Patterns B, C, and D, draw a 4⅛" square on graph paper. Divide the square as shown in Diagram 1, *above right.* The arrows on the diagram indicate the fabric grain directions for the triangle patterns. Make a template for the whole square (Pattern B), the large triangle (Pattern C), and the small triangle (Pattern D).

Make a 4⅛×7" rectangle template (Piece W).

Draw an 8¼" square. Divide the square as shown in Diagram 1.

Make a template for the entire square

here's a tip

When designing your own quilt, remember that using an even-numbered grid allows for symmetrical designs; odd-numbered grids can be oriented around a center point.

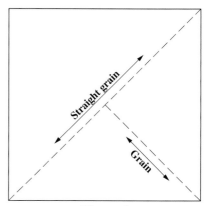

Diagram 1

(Pattern Y), the large triangle (Pattern X), and the small triangle (Pattern Z).

From cream fabric, cut:

- *12 of 8¼" square Y*
- *14 of triangle X with the long side of the triangle on fabric grain*
- *4 of triangle Z with the short sides of the triangle on the fabric grain*
- *164 of 4⅛" square B (8 for each block and 2 for each border corner)*
- *40 of triangle C with the long side of the triangle on the fabric grain (1 for each border unit and 2 for each corner unit)*
- *72 of triangle D with the short sides of the triangle on the fabric grain*
- *36–4⅛×7" rectangle W*

From medium blue No. 1 print fabric, cut:

- *196–A diamonds (page 117–8 for each block, 2 for each border unit, and 2 for each border corner)*

From light blue and medium blue No. 2 print fabrics, cut:

- *51–2½×45" strips, across the fabric width for diamonds*

kalona star quilt continued

From cream, light blue, medium blue No. 1, and medium blue No. 2. print fabrics, cut:

- *50–4½" squares from each fabric, for prairie point borders (measurement includes seam allowances)*

assemble the pieced diamonds

1. Sew pairs of medium blue No. 1 and light blue strips together lengthwise; press seam allowance toward medium blue fabric.
2. To cut diamonds, position Template A on a strip lengthwise with seam running through center of diamond. Mark four diamonds per strip; cut out diamonds, adding seam allowances. Make 204 pieced diamonds (160 for the blocks and 44 for the border).

assemble the blocks

1. When piecing, sew only on seam lines, avoiding seam allowances. Avoid stretching bias edges.
2. Referring to Diagram 2, sew eight pieced diamonds into a star. Position diamonds consistently so they are shaded as in the diagram.

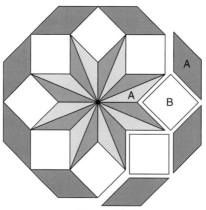

Diagram 2

3. Set a B square into each opening around the outside of the star. Set blue print diamonds into the spaces between squares around the star.
4. Repeat Steps 2 and 3 to make 20 star blocks.
5. To make a single block that will not be joined to other blocks, cut four Z triangles and sew them to blue print A diamonds to square off the block.

assemble the quilt top

1. Lay out the blocks in five rows with four blocks in each row. To make one row, join four blocks by stitching blue print diamonds together. Join rows together by attaching large Y squares between the rows.
2. Sew a Z triangle into the four corners of the quilt. Set in X triangles into the openings along the outer edges.

assemble and add the borders

1. Referring to Diagram 3, sew two pieced diamonds together. Set a C triangle into the opening between the diamonds. Attach a D triangle to opposite sides of the diamonds to form a rectangle. Make 36 border units from pieced diamonds.

Diagram 3

2. Make 28 border units similarly with pairs of blue print A diamonds.

116

3. For the side borders, alternate five pieced diamond border units with four blue print border units, placing a W rectangle at each end and between each border unit.

4. Referring to Diagram 4, sew a D triangle to medium blue print A diamond as shown in the portion indicated with a heavy line; make two D/A units and two reverse D/A units. Sew a D/A unit to one end and a reverse D/A unit to the opposite end of both side borders. Sew side borders to quilt top.

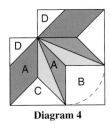

Diagram 4

5. To make the top and bottom borders, alternate four pieced diamond border units with three blue print border units, placing a W rectangle at each end and between each border unit.

6. Referring to Diagram 4, sew border corners from two pieced diamonds, one blue print A diamond, two C triangles, one B square, and two D triangles. Make two border corners and two reverse border corners.

7. Sew a border corner to one end and a reverse border corner to the opposite end of the top and bottom borders. Sew the borders to the quilt. Round off the B corner squares as indicated by the dotted line in Diagram 4.

assemble the prairie points

1. Fold a 4½" square in half diagonally so it forms a triangle and press. Fold the triangle in half to form a smaller triangle; press. Repeat to make 200 prairie points, 50 from each fabric.

2. Sew the prairie points onto the quilt top, alternating fabrics. Place the raw edges of the triangles even with the edge of the quilt and the tips toward the center of the quilt, overlapping triangles.

complete the quilt

Trim seam allowance to ¼" and press. Turn the edges of the quilt top to the wrong side and press so the prairie points are away from the center of the quilt. Layer the quilt top, batting, and backing according to the instructions in Quilter's Primer beginning on *page 179.* Quilt as desired.

To finish the prairie point edge, trim batting even with the edge of the quilt top. Trim backing, leaving ¼" beyond the quilt top. Turn under raw edge of the quilt back and slip-stitch in place.

Kalona Star Pattern A

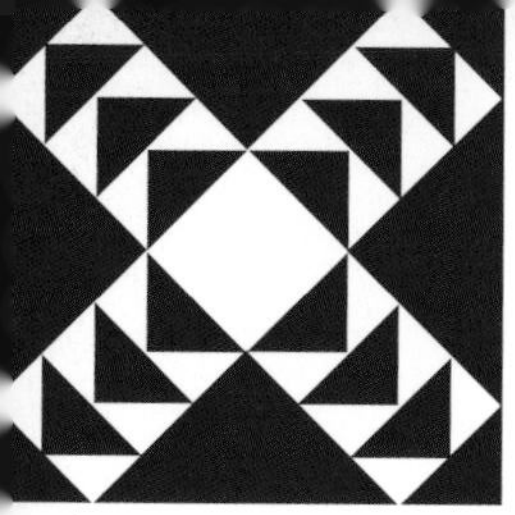

shaded crossroads

Here's a wonderful example of using elementary line drawings to expand your designing capabilities. Use squares and triangles for the blocks and quilt with a basic repeated floral design to create a winning quilt.

materials

1⅛ yards of blue print for blocks and borders
1 yard of solid royal blue for blocks and binding
1 yard of hand-dyed light gray print for blocks
¼ yard of solid dark gray for blocks
4–18×22" pieces (fat quarters) of hand-dyed teal print in a gradation (light, medium, medium-dark, and dark)
48" square of quilt batting

Finished quilt: 41½×41½
Finished block: 3 square

Quantities specified are for 44/45"-wide 100% cotton fabrics. All measurements include a ¼" seam allowance unless otherwise stated.

cut the fabrics

To make the best use of your fabrics, cut the pieces in the order that follows. These border strip measurements are mathematically correct. If desired, cut the border strips longer than specified to allow for possible sewing differences.

From blue print, cut:
- *2–2×33½" inner border strips*
- *2–2×36½" inner border strips*
- *4–2½×36½" outer border strips*
- *4–2½" squares for outer border*
- *30–3⅞" squares, cutting each in half diagonally for a total of 60 triangles*

From solid royal blue, cut:
- *11–1½×42" strips*
- *5–2½×42" binding strips*

From hand-dyed light gray print, cut:
- *8–1½×42" strips*
- *2–1¼×38" middle border strips*
- *2–1¼×36½" middle border strips*
- *8–1¼×2½" rectangles for outer border*

From solid dark gray, cut:
- *5–1½×42" strips*

From hand-dyed light teal print, cut:
- *5–3⅞" squares, cutting each in half diagonally for a total of 10 triangles*

From hand-dyed medium teal print, cut:
- *10–3⅞" squares, cutting each in half diagonally for a total of 20 triangles*

From hand-dyed medium-dark teal print, cut:
- *10–3⅞" squares, cutting each in half diagonally for a total of 20 triangles*

From hand-dyed dark teal print, cut:
- *5–3⅞" squares, cutting each in half diagonally for a total of 10 triangles*

assemble the nine-patch blocks

1. Aligning long edges, sew together one 1½×42" solid dark gray strip, one 1½×42" solid royal blue strip, and one 1½×42" light gray print strip to make a Strip Set A (see Diagram 1). Press the seam allowances toward the solid royal blue strip. Repeat to make a total of five of Strip Set A.

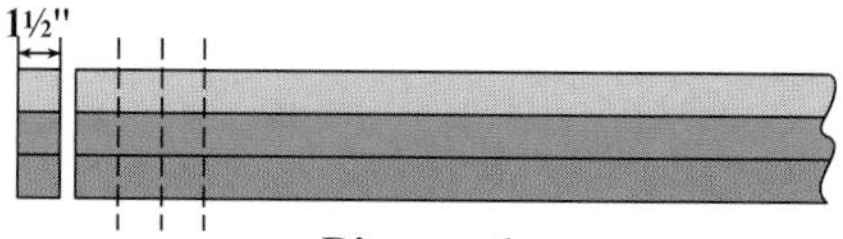

Diagram 1
Strip Set A

here's a tip
Many quilt patterns list pieces in the order in which they should be cut to avoid either waste or shortage of fabric.

shaded crossroads continued

2. Cut the five strip sets into a total of 122 segments, each 1½" wide.

3. Sew together one 1½×42" light gray print strip and two 1½×42" solid royal blue strips to make a Strip Set B (see Diagram 2). Press the seam allowances toward the solid royal blue strips. Repeat to make a total of three of Strip Set B.

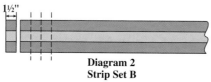

Diagram 2
Strip Set B

4. Cut the three strip sets into a total of 61 segments, each 1½" wide.

5. Referring to Diagram 3 for placement, sew together two Strip Set A segments and one Strip Set B segment to make a Nine-Patch block. Press the seam allowances in one direction. The pieced Nine-Patch block should measure 3½" square, including the seam allowances. Repeat to make a total of 61 Nine-Patch blocks.

Diagram 3

assemble the triangle-squares

1. Sew together one blue print triangle and one teal print triangle to make a triangle-square (see Diagram 4). Press the seam allowance toward the blue print triangle. The pieced triangle-square should measure 3½" square, including the seam allowances.

2. Repeat Step 1 with the remaining

Diagram 4

blue print and teal print triangles to make a total of 60 triangle-squares.

assemble the quilt center

1. Referring to the photograph, *opposite*, lay out the 61 Nine-Patch blocks and the 60 triangle-squares in 11 rows of 11 blocks each. If desired, position the triangle-squares so the rows shade from light to dark.

2. Sew together the squares in each row. Press the seam allowances in one direction, alternating the direction with each row. Join the rows to complete the quilt center. Press the seam allowances in one direction. The pieced quilt center should measure 33½" square, including the seam allowances.

assemble the borders

1. Sew a 2×33½" blue print inner border strip to the top and bottom edges of the pieced quilt center. Join one 2×36½" blue print inner border strip to each side edge of the pieced quilt center. Press all seam allowances toward the blue print borders.

2. Sew a 1¼×36½" light gray print middle border strip to the top and bottom edges of the pieced quilt center. Join a 1¼×38" light gray print middle border strip to each side edge of the pieced quilt center. Press all seam allowances toward the light gray borders.

3. Sew a 1¼×2½" light gray print rectangle to each end of the 2½×36½" blue print outer border strips to make four outer border units. Press the seam allowances toward the blue print strips.

4. Sew an outer border unit to the top and bottom edges of the pieced quilt center. Press the seam allowances toward the outer border units.

5. Sew a 2½" blue print square to each end of the remaining outer border units. Press the seam allowances toward the blue print squares.

6. Sew a pieced outer border unit to each side edge of the pieced quilt center to complete the quilt top. Press the seam allowances toward the outer borders.

complete the quilt

Layer the quilt top, batting, and backing according to the instructions in Quilter's Primer, beginning on *page 179*. Quilt as desired. The sample displays a machine-quilted four-leaf design in each triangle-square and a vine of leaves in the border.

Use the 2½×42" solid royal blue strips to bind the quilt according to the instructions in Quilter's Primer.

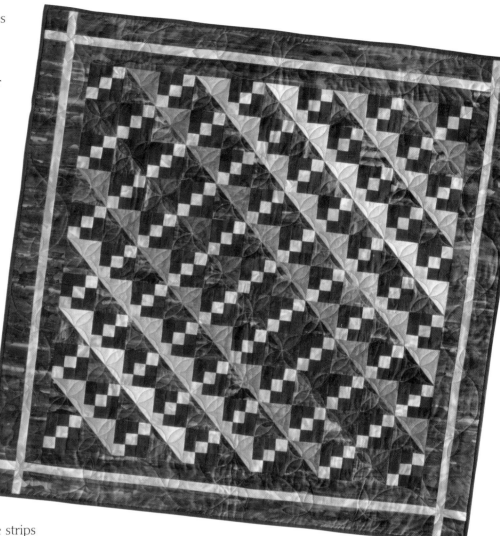

Make a Multicolor Version of This Two-Color Quilt

Create this project in another colorway using a combination of pinks. The green-and-pink leaf print in the outer border pulls all the colors together.

ohio blue leaf quilt

The sprightly quilt pattern from which the Ohio Blue Leaf design is lifted features sky blue calico appliquéd on a white quilted background—one of the all-time favorite color schemes of quiltmakers past and present.

materials

6½ yards of white fabric
2½ yards of blue fabric
5 yards of backing fabric
88" square of quilt batting

Finished quilt: 82" square

Quantities specified are for 44/45"-wide 100% cotton fabrics. All measurements include a ¼" seam allowance unless otherwise stated.

instructions

This quilt is constructed of sixteen 17"-square pattern blocks. Each block has a crisscross stem with 24 appliquéd leaves.

make master pattern

On brown paper draw a 17" square. Add ¼-inch seam allowances. Referring to the photograph, *opposite*, draw two ½"-wide stems in an X shape on the 17" square.

Using the full-size pattern, *below*, make a leaf template. Trace leaf shapes onto the master pattern, positioning leaves as shown in the photograph.

cut the fabrics

Trace 384 leaves onto blue fabric, allowing at least ½" between leaves; cut out the leaves, adding ¼" seam allowances. Clip curves and baste under seam allowances.

cut the stems

From blue fabric, cut out thirty-two 1×18½" stems. Turn under ¼" seam allowances along the sides of each stem; press.

cut the border strips

From white fabric, cut four 7½×82½" border strips.

assemble the blocks

1. Cut out sixteen 18" blocks from white fabric. Pin stems onto white blocks and slip-stitch in place.
2. Pin leaves to stems. Baste; then hand appliqué in place. Repeat until all 16 blocks are completed. Remove basting.
3. Trim blocks to 17½" square.
4. Arrange completed blocks in four rows of four blocks. Sew together. Sew border strips to the appliquéd blocks, mitering corners. Piece backing to size.

complete the quilt

Layer the quilt top, batting, and backing according to the instructions in Quilter's Primer, beginning on *page 179*. Quilt as desired. Bind quilt according to instructions in Quilter's Primer.

here's a tip

To create a mirror image of a template with fabric, flip the template over before tracing it onto the fabric.

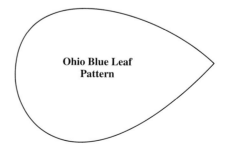

Ohio Blue Leaf Pattern

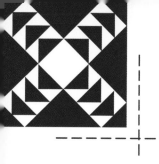

birds in the air

Hundreds of triangles in three sizes create an energized visual that resembles a flock of soaring birds. The solid blue at the edges creates a calming border for the detailed quilt design.

materials

3½ yards of cream print for blocks and borders

12—¾-yard pieces of assorted blue prints for blocks, borders, and binding

4⅞ yards of backing fabric

74×86" of quilt batting

Finished quilt: 68×80"
Finished block: 6" square

Quantities specified are for 44/45"-wide 100% cotton fabrics. All measurements include a ¼" seam allowance unless otherwise stated.

cut the fabrics

To make the best use of your fabrics, cut the pieces in the order that follows.

From cream print, cut:

- *12—2½×42" border strips*
- *368—2⅞" squares, cutting each in half diagonally for a total of 736 triangles*

From *each* of the 12 assorted blue prints, cut:

- *2—2½×42" strips for borders and binding*
- *4—6⅞" squares, cutting each in half diagonally for a total of 8 large triangles (you'll have 12 leftover triangles from the total 384 triangles)*
- *11—2⅞" squares, cutting each in half diagonally for a total of 22 small triangles (you'll have 12 leftover triangles from the total 264 triangles)*
- *3—5¼" squares, cutting each diagonally twice in an X for a total of 12 medium triangles (you'll have 28 leftover triangles from the total 144 triangles.)*

assemble the blocks

1. For one block gather six cream print triangles, and three small triangles and one large triangle from the same blue print.

birds in the air continued

2. Sew together one cream print triangle and one small blue print triangle to make a triangle-square (see Diagram 1). The pieced triangle-square should measure 2½" square, including the seam allowances. Repeat to make a total of three triangle-squares.

Diagram 1

Diagram 2

3. Referring to Diagram 2 for placement, join the three triangle-squares with the remaining three cream print triangles.

4. Sew the large blue print triangle to the pieced cream and blue triangles (see Diagram 3) to make a Birds in the Air block. Press the seam allowances toward the large blue print triangle. The pieced Birds in the Air block should measure 6½" square, including seam allowances.

Diagram 3

5. Repeat Steps 1 through 4 to make seven blocks from *each* of the 12 blue print for a total of 84 blocks.

assemble the quilt center

1. Referring to the photograph, *page 124,* lay out the pieced blocks in 10 rows of eight blocks each. Set aside four blocks to use in the border. If desired, alternate the position of the blocks to create further interest.

2. Sew together the blocks in each row. Press the seam allowances in one direction, alternating the direction with each row. Join the rows to complete the quilt center. Press the seam allowances in one direction. The pieced quilt center should measure 48½x60½", including seam allowances.

assemble the borders

1. Referring to Diagram 4, with right sides facing, sew together a cream print triangle and a medium blue print triangle. Join a second cream print triangles to the blue print triangle to make a Flying Geese unit. Press all seam allowances toward the cream print triangles. The pieced Flying Geese unit should measure 2½x4½", including the seam allowances.

Diagram 4

2. Repeat Step 1 to make a total of 116 Flying Geese units.

3. Cut and piece the 2½x42" cream print strips to make the following:
- 2–2½x64½" border strips
- 2–2½x60½" border strips
- 4–2½x52½" border strips

4. Sew a 2½x60½" cream print border strip to each side edge of the pieced quilt center. Press the seam allowances toward the cream print borders. Join a 2½x52½" cream print border strip to the top and bottom edges of the pieced quilt center. Press the seam allowances toward the cream print borders. The pieced quilt center should now measure 52½×64½", including seam allowances.

5. Sew together 32 Flying Geese units in a vertical row. Press the seam allowances in one direction. Sew a 2½×64½" cream print border strip to a long edge of the Flying Geese row to make a side pieced border unit. Press the seam allowance toward the cream print strip. Repeat to make a second side pieced border unit.

6. Sew the side pieced border units to the side edges of the pieced quilt center. Press the seam allowances toward the quilt center.

7. Sew together 26 Flying Geese units in a horizontal row. Press the seam allowances in one direction. Sew a 2½×52½" cream print border strip to a long edge of the Flying Geese row. Press the seam allowance toward the cream print strip. Sew a pieced Bird in the Air block to each end of the strip to make a top pieced border unit. Press the seam allowance toward the cream print strip. Repeat to make a bottom pieced border unit.

8. Sew the top and bottom pieced border units to the top and bottom edges of the pieced quilt center. Press the seam allowances toward the quilt center. The quilt center should now measure 64½×76½", including seam allowances.

9. Cut and piece the 2½×42" blue print strips to make the following:
   • 2–2½×76½" outer border strips
   • 2–2½×68½" outer border strips

10. Sew a 2½×76½" blue print outer border strip to each side edge of the pieced quilt center. Then add a blue print 2½×68½" outer border strip to the top and bottom edges of the pieced

quilt center to complete the quilt top. Press all seam allowances toward the blue print outer borders.

complete the quilt

Layer the quilt top, batting, and backing according to Quilter's Primer, beginning on *page 179*. Quilt as desired. The sample shows machine quilting in an allover stippling pattern.

Use the remaining 2½"-wide blue print strips to bind the quilt according to the instructions in Quilter's Primer.

Make a Multicolor Version of This Two-Color Quilt

Use your favorite fabrics to stitch a 12-block variation in two long rows. This size is ideal for a table runner.

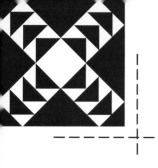

double irish chain quilt

With basic rotary cutting and strip piecing, even first-time quiltmakers succeed at accomplishing this classic two-color jewel with ease.

materials

3–1-yard pieces of assorted blue
   prints for blocks
5¼ yards of muslin for blocks, sawtooth
   borders, and pieced borders
½ yard of blue print No. 1 for
   sawtooth borders
⅝ yard of blue print No. 2 for
   pieced borders
¾ yard of solid blue for binding
7½ yards of backing fabric
89×97" of quilt batting

Finished quilt: 83×91"
Finished block: 14" square

Quantities specified are for 44/45"-wide 100% cotton fabrics. All measurements include a ¼" seam allowance. Sew with right sides together unless otherwise indicated.

cut the fabrics

To make the best use of your fabrics, cut the pieces in the order that follows.

From assorted blue prints, cut:
• 33–2½×42" strips

double irish chain quilt continued

From muslin, cut:
- *15–10½" squares*
- *4–6½×42" strips*
- *37–2½×42" strips*
- *3–3⅞×42" strips*

From blue print No. 1, cut:
- *3–3⅞×42" strips*

From blue print No. 2, cut:
- *9–2×42" strips*

From solid blue, cut:
- *9–2½×42" binding strips*

assemble the checkerboard blocks

1. Sew together four 2½×42"assorted blue print strips and three 2½×42" muslin strips to make a Strip Set A (see Diagram 1). Press the seam allowances toward the blue print strips. Repeat to make a total of four of Strip Set A.

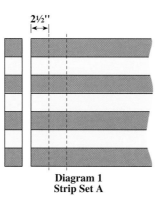

Diagram 1
Strip Set A

2. Cut the strip sets into a total of sixty 2½"-wide Strip Set A segments.

3. Sew together three assorted 2½×42" blue print strips and four 2½×42" muslin strips to make a Strip Set B (see Diagram 2). Press the seam allowances toward the blue print strips. Repeat to make a total of three of Strip Set B.

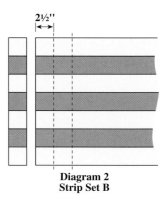

Diagram 2
Strip Set B

4. Cut the strip sets into a total of forty-five 2½"-wide Strip Set B segments.

5. Sew together four Strip Set A segments and three Strip Set B segments to make a Checkerboard block (see Diagram 3). Press the seam allowances in one direction. The Checkerboard block should measure 14½" square, including the seam allowances.

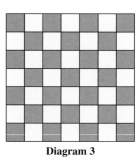

Diagram 3

6. Repeat Step 5 to make a total of 15 checkerboard blocks.

assemble the setting blocks

1. Sew together two assorted 2½×42" blue print strips and one 6½×42" muslin strip to make a Strip Set C (see Diagram 4). Press the seam allowances toward the blue print strips. Repeat to make a total of two of Strip Set C.

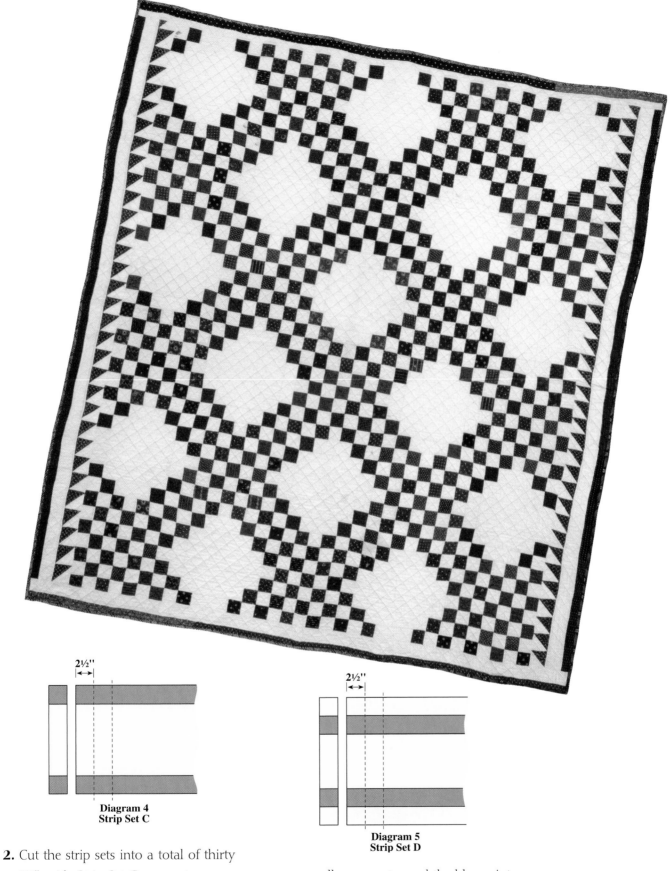

Diagram 4
Strip Set C

2½"

Diagram 5
Strip Set D

2½"

2. Cut the strip sets into a total of thirty 2½"-wide Strip Set C segments.

3. Sew together two assorted 2½×42" blue print strips, two 2½×42" muslin strips, and one 6½×42" muslin strip to make a Strip Set D (see Diagram 5). Press the

seam allowances toward the blue print strips. Repeat to make a total of two of Strip Set D.

4. Cut the strip sets into a total of thirty 2½"-wide Strip Set D segments.

5. Sew a Strip Set C segment to the top and bottom edges of a 10½" muslin square (see Diagram 6). Join a Strip Set D segment to each side edge of the muslin square to make a setting block. Press the seam allowances toward the strip set segments. The setting block should measure 14½" square, including the seam allowances.

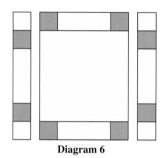

Diagram 6

6. Repeat Step 5 to make a total of 15 setting blocks.

assemble the quilt center

1. Referring to the photograph, *page 131,* lay out the blocks in six horizontal rows of five blocks each, alternating the Checkerboard and setting blocks.

2. Sew together the blocks in each row. Press the seam allowances toward the setting blocks. Then join the rows to make the quilt center. Press the seam allowances in one direction. The pieced quilt center should measure 70½×84½", including the seam allowances.

assemble the sawtooth border

1. Pair each 3⅞×42" blue print strip with a 3⅞×42" muslin strip; layer them with right sides together. Cut the layered strips into a total of twenty-eight 3⅞"-wide segments (see Diagram 7).

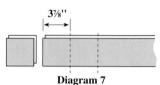

Diagram 7

Cut the layered squares in half diagonally for a total of 56 triangle pairs. Stitch ¼" from the diagonal edge of each triangle pair and press to make a total of 56 triangle-squares (see Diagram 8). Each triangle-square should measure 3½" square, including seam allowances.

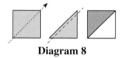

Diagram 8

2. Sew together 28 triangle-squares and press to make a sawtooth border strip; repeat. Sew the sawtooth border strips to each side edge of the pieced quilt center. Press the seam allowances toward the pieced quilt center. [Note: The sawtooth borders on the photographed antique quilt, *page 131,* was inconsistently pieced. These instructions provide you with the measurements to make the border fit correctly.

here's a tip

If the seam allowances are inconsistent and one pieced unit is slightly longer than the other, place the longer unit on the bottom against the machine bed. The feed dogs ease in a bit of the extra fullness when you sew the pieces together.

assemble the pieced border

These measurements for border strips are mathematically correct. Before cutting the strips, measure your quilt top and adjust the lengths as necessary.

1. Cut and piece the remaining nine 2½×42" muslin strips to make the following:
   - *2−2½×84½" border strips*
   - *2−2½×83½" border strips*

2. Cut and piece the 2×42" blue print No. 2 strips to make the following:
   - *2−2×84½" border strips*
   - *2−2×83½" border strips*

3. Sew together a 2½×84½" muslin border strip and a 2×84½" blue print border strip to make a side pieced border unit. Press the seam allowance toward the blue print strip. Repeat to make a second side pieced border unit.

4. Sew one side pieced border unit to each side edge of the quilt center, placing the muslin strip next to the quilt center. Press the seam allowances toward the borders.

5. Sew together a 2½×83½" muslin border strip and a 2×83½" blue print border strip to make a top pieced border unit. Press the seam allowance toward the blue print strip. Repeat to make a bottom pieced border unit.

6. Sew a pieced border unit to the top and bottom edges of the quilt center to complete the quilt top. Press the seam allowances toward the borders.

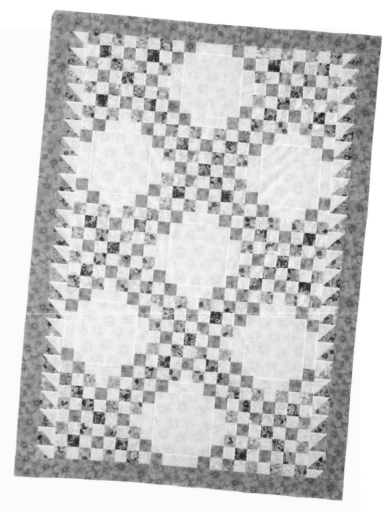

Pretty in Pink

To lend some pizzazz to your spring decorating, quilt a large wall hanging using a luscious pink palette.

complete the quilt

Layer the quilt top, batting, and backing according to the instructions in Quilter's Primer, which begins on *page 179*. Quilt as desired. The antique quilt shown on page 131 was quilted diagonally through all squares to make an even squared grid in the open muslin squares.

Use the 2½×42" solid blue strips to bind the quilt according to the instructions in Quilter's Primer.

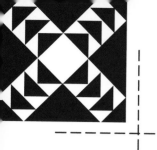

snow crystals quilt

Find a new way to use the traditional Dresden Plate block with this quilt that changes the placement of the block's units. The arrangement resembles snowflakes fluttering down the quilt, overlapping here and there as they do in nature.

 **pattern sheet**

materials

2¾ yards of dark blue fern print for blocks and outer borders

3¼ yards of solid white for blocks, inner borders, and binding

½ yard of blue print for blocks

2⅞ yards of backing fabric

51×71" of quilt batting

Finished quilt: 46½×66½"

Finished block: 4" square

Quantities specified are for 44/45"-wide 100% cotton fabrics. All measurements include a ¼" seam allowance unless otherwise stated.

cut the fabrics

To make the best use of your fabrics, cut the pieces in the order that follows. The border strips are cut the length of the fabric (parallel to the selvage). You may wish to cut the border strips extra long to allow for sewing differences, then trim them once they're added to the quilt top.

The patterns are on the Pattern Sheet. To make templates of the pattern pieces, follow the instructions in Quilter's Primer, beginning on *page 179*.

beginning on *page 179*.

here's a tip

Clip threads as you go. It makes piecing easier when you don't have to worry about extra threads.

From dark blue fern print, cut:

- 2–3×62" outer border strips
- 2–3×47" outer border strips
- 2–16½×4½" rectangles
- 2–8½×12½" rectangles
- 11–8½" squares

- 2–8½×4½" rectangles
- 82–4½" squares

From solid white, cut:

- 455 of Pattern A
- 2–1¼×60½" inner border strips
- 2–1¼×42" inner border strips
- 6–2¼×42" binding strips

From blue print, cut:

- 8 of Pattern B
- 59 of Pattern C

assemble dresden plate units

1. With the right side inside, fold each solid white A piece in half lengthwise (see Diagram 1). Using a short stitch length, sew ¼" from the top edge of each folded A piece.

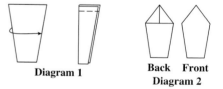

Diagram 1   **Back Front**
Diagram 2

2. Turn each folded and stitched A piece right side out to make 455 Dresden Plate points (see Diagram 2); press.

3. Sew together five Dresden Plate points to make a Dresden Plate unit (see Diagram 3). Press the seam allowances open. Repeat to make a total of 91 Dresden Plate units.

Diagram 3

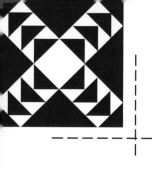

assemble the small dresden plate blocks

1. Position a Dresden Plate unit on a 4½" dark blue fern print square, tacking the unit in place at the inner points (see the red dots in Diagram 4).

Diagram 4

2. Using thread in a color that matches the fabric, appliqué a blue print C piece at the base of the Dresden Plate unit to complete the small Dresden Plate block.

3. Trim the dark blue fern print from behind the appliquéd center C piece.

4. Repeat Steps 1 through 3 to make a total of 59 small Dresden Plate blocks.

assemble the large dresden plate blocks

1. Sew together four Dresden Plate units to make a Dresden Plate circle; press the seam allowances open. Repeat to make a total of eight Dresden Plate circles.

2. Center a Dresden Plate circle on a 8½" dark blue fern print square; tack in place as before.

3. Using thread in a color that matches the fabric, appliqué a blue print center B circle in the center of the Dresden Plate circle to complete a large Dresden Plate block.

4. Repeat Steps 2 and 3 to make a total of eight large Dresden Plate blocks.

assemble the quilt center

1. Referring to the Quilt Assembly Diagram, *opposite*, for placement, lay out the small Dresden Plate blocks, the large Dresden Plate blocks, and the remaining dark blue fern print squares and rectangles in sections.

2. Sew together the pieces in each section. Then join the sections to make the quilt center. The pieced quilt center should measure 40½×60½", including the seam allowances.

assemble the borders

1. Sew a 1¼×60½" solid white inner border strip to each side edge of the quilt center. Press the seam allowances toward the white borders. Then sew a solid 1¼×42" white inner border strip to the top and bottom edges of the quilt center. Press the seam allowances toward the white borders.

2. Sew a 3×62" dark blue fern print outer border strip to each side edge of the quilt center. Sew a 3×47" dark blue fern print outer border strip to the top and bottom edges of the quilt center. Press all seam allowances toward the dark blue fern print border.

complete the quilt

Layer the quilt top, batting, and backing according to the instructions in Quilter's Primer, beginning on *page 179*.

Quilt as desired. The sample is machine quilted with rayon thread to add sparkle. The print of the blue fabric

8½" square

16½" x 4½"

8½" x 12½"

8½" x 4½"

8½" x 12½"

8½" square

8½" x 4½"

16½" x 4½"

8½" square

Quilt Assembly Diagram

Make a Multicolor Version of This Two-Color Quilt

Dark colors lend themselves to late summer's sunflowers and coneflowers on this wall hanging. Note how the design of the outer flowers differs from the quilt, giving the block a polished look.

here's a tip

When cutting appliqué foundations, stay at least ½" away from the selvage edge, which is tightly woven. A rippled edge forms on your foundation if you cut too near it.

was followed with free-motion quilting. Also quilted in the design, are the creator's name, the name of the quilt, and the date the quilt was made.

Use the 2¼×42" solid white strips to bind the quilt according to the instructions in Quilter's Primer.

Permanent dyes made a wider range of color fabrics easy to find in the mid–1800s.  This chapter highlights quilts that use yellow, peach, green, and pink fabrics in combination with crisp white and muslin tones to showcase their glorious color.

dolley madison's star
This antique quilt is fresh and cheery—perfect for summertime bedding. Re-create the sunshiny pattern using the instructions on *pages 150–153*.

hawaiian leaves

When studying this 1930s quilt, Tahitian-style appliqué teachers noted the pattern appears to be an adaptation of an unnamed Hawaiian design. The quiltmaker likely reduced it in size, then stitched it symmetrically, joining the sashing and border.

 **pattern sheet**

materials

5¾ yards of solid dark peach for appliqués, sashing, checkerboard, and border

6½ yards of solid white for block foundations, sashing, checkerboard unit, borders, and binding

Sharp #11 appliqué needles

18" square of tracing paper

98" square of quilt batting

6 yards of backing fabric

Finished quilt: 92" square

Finished block: 33¾" square

Quantities specified are for 44/45"-wide 100% cotton fabrics. All measurements include a ¼" seam allowance unless otherwise stated.

cut the fabrics

To make the best use of your fabrics, cut the pieces in the order that follows. To make templates from the patterns found on the Pattern Sheet, follow the instructions in Quilter's Primer beginning on *page 179.*

From solid dark peach, cut:
- *4—34¼" appliqué squares*
- *12—3×34¼" sashing strips*
- *12—3" checkerboard squares*
- *84 of Pattern A (Pattern Sheet)*

From solid white, cut:
- *40" square, cutting enough 2½"-wide bias strips to total approximately 375" in length (for specific*

instructions on cutting bias strips see Quilter's Primer)
- *4—34¼" foundation squares*
- *8—3×34¼" sashing strips*
- *13—3" checkerboard squares*
- *4 of Pattern A (Pattern Sheet)*
- *80 of Pattern B (Pattern Sheet)*

appliqué the blocks

1. For one block you'll need one 34¼"solid dark peach square and one 34¼" solid white square.

2. Referring to the Folding Diagram, fold the dark peach square in half, forming a rectangle. Fold the rectangle in half, forming a square. Then fold the square in half diagonally, forming a triangle. To create placement guidelines, firmly press the folded edges of the triangle. Repeat with the white square.

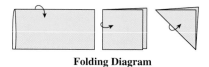

Folding Diagram

3. Lay the tracing paper atop the Hawaiian Leaves Appliqué Design on the Pattern Sheet; trace the design.

4. Place the traced pattern atop the folded dark peach triangle, aligning the pattern's dashed lines with the triangle's folded edges. Thoroughly pin the pattern to the fabric, placing pins only inside the gray design area.

5. Cutting on the solid lines only, cut through all eight layers of dark peach fabric to create the appliqué design.

6. Unfold both the foundation square and the appliqué design. Lay the appliqué design atop the white foundation square, matching all the placement guidelines.

7. Using large basting stitches, sew the appliqué design to the foundation square ½" from the raw edges.

8. Using a thread color that matches the fabric, appliqué the design to the foundation, turning under the raw edges with your needle as you stitch.

9. Repeat Steps 1 through 8 to make a total of four appliquéd blocks.

assemble the sashing units

1. For one sashing unit you'll need three 3×34¼" dark peach sashing strips and two 3×34¼" white sashing strips.

2. Aligning long raw edges, sew together the sashing strips in a unit that begins and ends with a dark peach strip (refer to photograph, *opposite*, for placement). Press the seam allowances toward the dark peach strips. The pieced sashing unit should measure 13×34¼", including the seam allowances.

3. Repeat Steps 1 and 2 for a total of four sashing units.

assemble the checkerboard unit

1. For the checkerboard unit you'll need the twelve 3" dark peach squares and the thirteen 3" white squares.

2. Lay out the squares in five horizontal rows of five squares each, alternating the colors (see the photograph, *opposite*, for placement).

3. Sew together the horizontal rows. Press the seam allowances toward the dark peach squares. Then join the rows. Press the seam allowances in one direction. The pieced checkerboard unit should measure 13" square, including the seam allowances.

assemble the quilt top

Referring to the photograph, lay out the appliquéd blocks, sashing units, and checkerboard unit in rows. Sew together the pieces in each row. Press the seam allowances toward the sashing units. Join the rows. The pieced quilt top should measure 80½" square, including the seam allowances.

assemble the borders

1. For one border unit you'll need 21 dark peach A pieces and 20 white B pieces. Sew together the pieces, alternating the colors. Press the seam allowances toward the dark peach A pieces. Repeat for a total of four border units.

2. Sew one border unit to the top edge of the pieced quilt top and one to the bottom edge. Avoid stitching into the seam allowances at the corners of the pieced quilt top. Press the seam allowances toward the border units.

3. Sew a white A piece to each end of the remaining two border units, stitching only to the marked dot.

4. Sew the remaining border units to the side edges of the pieced quilt top, sewing only to the dot marked on the end white A pieces. Avoid stitching into

here's a tip

Numbers on appliqué pieces are important. They indicate the appliquéing sequence and designate the right sides of the templates.

the seam allowances at the corners of the pieced quilt top. Sew the side borders to the top and bottom borders at the corners.

complete the quilt

Layer the quilt top, batting, and backing according to the instructions in the Quilter's Primer beginning on *page 179*.

Although this antique quilt is hand-quilted with a ½"-wide crosshatch, full-size Hawaiian quilts traditionally are echo-quilted every ½" around the appliqué design with white thread. Bind the quilt according to the instructions in Quilter's Primer with 2½"-wide white bias strips.

mariner's compass

Use paper foundation piecing to stay on course when assembling this project.
Follow the step-by-step photographs to consistently stitch the extremely sharp
points needed for this traditional pattern.

pattern sheet

materials

- *8⅞ yards of solid yellow for blocks, corner squares, and borders*
- *15 yards of muslin for blocks, corner squares, and borders*
- *⅞ yard of multicolor print for binding*
- *5" square of lightweight cardboard for template*
- *5½ yards of backing fabric*
- *77×100" of quilt batting; tracing paper*

Finished quilt: 71×95"
Finished block: 11" square

Quantities specified are for 44/45"-wide 100% cotton fabrics. All measurements include a ¼" seam allowance unless otherwise stated.

cut the fabrics

To make the best use of your fabrics, cut the pieces in the order that follows. To make templates of the pattern pieces, found on the Pattern Sheet, follow the instructions in Quilter's Primer beginning on *page 179.*

From solid yellow, cut:
- *1,728–1½×4" strips for blocks*
- *96 of Pattern C (Pattern Sheet)*
- *9–3×42" inner border strips*
- *4–1½×3" rectangles for outer border*

From muslin, cut:
- *1,920–1½×4" strips for blocks*
- *192 of Pattern B (Pattern Sheet)*
- *96 of Pattern C (Pattern Sheet)*
- *4–1½×42" outer border strips*
- *4–3" squares for inner border*

From multicolor print, cut:
- *9–2½×42" binding strips*

From lightweight cardboard, cut:
- *1 of Pattern D (Pattern Sheet)*

make the foundation papers

1. Using tracing paper and a pencil, trace Pattern A 24 times, as shown in Photo A on *page 147*, tracing all lines and numbers; leave at least 2" between tracings. Place each tracing on top of a stack of eight unmarked sheets of tracing paper. (Freezer paper and typing paper also work.) Staple each stack together once or twice on each edge (see Photo B on *page 147*).

2. Using a sewing machine with an unthreaded small-gauge needle set on 10 to 12 stitches per inch, sew each stack on the traced inner lines through all layers of paper. Avoid stitching on the traced outer line of the pattern.

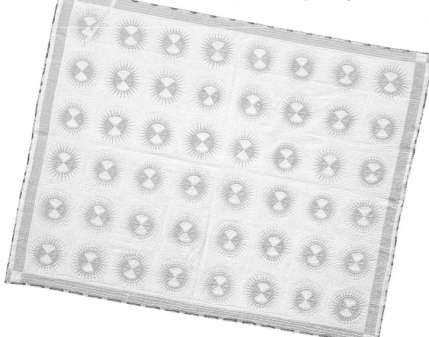

3. With scissors, cut each stack on the traced outer line for a total of 192 perforated foundation papers.

assemble the units

1. With right sides together, place a 1½×4" muslin strip atop a 1½×4" solid yellow strip. Put a perforated foundation paper on top of the muslin strip, positioning the strips so the right edges are a scant ¼" beyond the first stitching line and about ⅜" above the top of the arc (see Photo C, *opposite*). Sew on stitching line No. 1. *Note:* For photographic purposes black thread was used to stitch these sample pieces. When you sew, we recommend using a color that matches your fabric or a medium gray.

2. Trim the seam allowance to a scant ¼ inch. When sewing with dark colors, trim the seam allowance so the darker fabric does not show through the lighter fabric. Press the strips open; press the seam allowance toward the yellow strip (see Photo D). Trim the yellow strip to about ¼" beyond stitching line No. 2. Trim the strips even with the top and bottom edges of the foundation paper (see Photo E).

3. Align another 1½×4" muslin strip with the trimmed yellow piece so their right edges are about ¼" beyond stitching line No. 2. Sew along stitching line No. 2 (see Photo F). Trim the seam allowance if needed; press the seam allowance toward the muslin strip (see Photo G). Trim the second muslin strip even with the top and bottom edges of the foundation paper.

4. Continue joining alternating yellow and muslin strips and trimming in the same manner until the entire arc unit is pieced (see Photo H). With the blunt edge of a seam ripper, remove foundation paper.

5. Repeat Steps 1 through 4 to make a total of 192 pieced arcs.

assemble the blocks

1. With right sides together, pin the center top of a pieced arc to the center top of a muslin B piece (marked with Xs on the pattern). Then pin each end. Pin generously between each end and the center (see Photo I) to get a flat seam.

2. Using a ½" seam allowance, sew the pieces together along the top arc either by hand or machine, sewing a little to the right of the sewing line if necessary to ensure sharp points. (A ½" seam allowance is included on the outside edges of the arc unit to allow for any sewing variations.)

3. Hand-stitching allows you to check for a smooth seam as you stitch by turning the piece over occasionally to look at the back.

4. If you choose to machine-stitch, keep the pieced arc on top when you put the pieces under the presser foot. Work slowly, stop the machine often with the needle down, and adjust the sewing direction as needed.

5. Press the seam allowance toward the muslin B piece.

6. Repeat with the remaining pieced arcs and the remaining muslin B pieces.

7. Combine four Step 1 units to form a Mariner's Compass block (see Photo J).

here's a tip

When cutting an equilateral triangle, note that the ruler sometimes covers the shape you are cutting. It's easier and more efficient to move the ruler from one side of the shape to the other than to move the fabric strip or rotate the cutting mat.

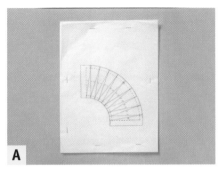

A

Trace Pattern A 24 times on tracing paper, tracing all of the lines and numbers. Leave at least 2 inches between the markings.

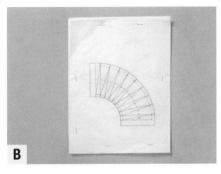

B

Place each tracing on top of a stack of unmarked sheets of tracing paper. Staple each stack together once or twice on each edge.

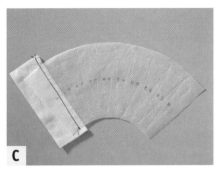

C

Put a perforated foundation paper on top of muslin strip. Position strips so right edges are a scant ¼" beyond first stitching line and about ⅜" above arc top.

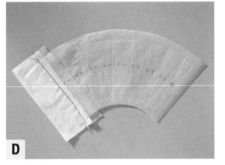

D

Press the strips open, pressing the seam allowance toward the yellow strip.

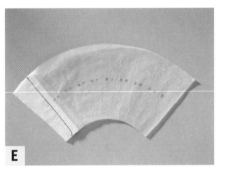

E

Trim the strips even with the top and bottom edges of the foundation paper.

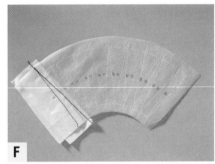

F

Sew along stitching line.

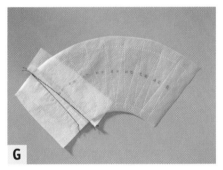

G

Trim the seam allowance if needed; press the seam allowance toward the muslin strip.

H

Continue adding strips and trimming in the same manner until the entire arc unit is pieced.

I

Pin generously between each end and the center.

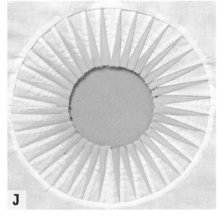

J

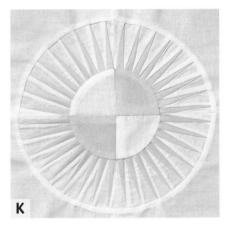

K

Combine four Step 1 units (far left) to form a Mariner's Compass block.

Appliqué an inner circle (left) over the center of each block.

Repeat for a total of 48 blocks. After assembling, trim each Mariner's Compass block to measure 11½" square, including the seam allowances.

8. To assemble the inner circles, pair each muslin C piece with a solid yellow C piece; sew together. Sew together the pairs to make a total of 48 inner circles.

9. Make a basting stitch a scant ¼" from the raw edge of each inner circle. Position the cardboard D template on the wrong side of an inner circle. Pull up the basting stitches, spread the gathers out evenly, and gently press to make a smooth edge. Tie the thread ends and remove the cardboard. Repeat with the remaining inner circles.

10. Appliqué an inner circle over the center of each block (see Photo K).

assemble the quilt top

Referring to the photograph on *page 144* for placement, lay out the blocks in eight horizontal rows of six blocks each. Sew together the blocks in each row. Press the seam allowances in one direction, alternating the direction with each row. Then join the rows. Press the seam allowances in one direction. The pieced quilt center should measure 66½×88½", including the seam allowances.

assemble the borders

1. Cut and piece the 3×42"solid yellow strips to measure as follows:
   • 2–3×88½" inner border strips
   • 2–3×66½" inner border strips

2. Sew one 3×66½" solid yellow inner border strip to the top edge of the

pieced quilt top and one to the bottom edge. Sew a 3" muslin square to each end of the 3×88½" solid yellow inner border strips. Press the seam allowances toward the muslin squares. Join one border strip to each side edge of the pieced quilt top. Press all seam allowances toward the yellow borders.

3. Cut and piece the 1½×42" muslin strips to measure as follows:
   • 2–1½×66½" strips

4 Sew a 1½×3" solid yellow rectangle to each end of the muslin strips. Sew one strip to the top edge of the pieced quilt top and one to the bottom edge. Press the seam allowances toward the muslin borders.

complete the quilt

Layer the quilt top, batting, and backing according to the instructions in Quilter's Primer beginning on *page 179*. Quilt as desired. Use the 2½×42" multicolor print strips to bind the quilt according to the instructions in Quilter's Primer.

PILLOW TALK
materials

2½ yards of solid yellow; 1½ yards of muslin
2–12" square pillow forms; standard bed pillow

cut the fabrics

From solid yellow, cut:
   • *2–19½×16" rectangles*
   • *2–2×27½" border strips*
   • *4–1½×11½" border strips*
   • *156–1½×4" strips for blocks*
   • *12 of Pattern B (Pattern Sheet)*
   • *8 of Pattern C (Pattern Sheet)*

here's a tip
Always cut border pieces on the straight grain of the fabric, rather than the bias, because the bias has give, and border with give will cause the quilt to stretch out of shape over time.

- 4–3" squares for border
- 4–1½" squares for border
- 2–13½" squares

From muslin, cut:
- 2–3×22½" border strips
- 2–3×11½" border strips
- 4–1½×11½" border strips
- 148–1½×4" strips for blocks
- 4 of Pattern B (Pattern Sheet)
- 8 of Pattern C (Pattern Sheet)
- 4–1½" squares for border

assemble the blocks

Referring to the assembly instructions, *pages 146–148*, make one Mariner's Compass block. Then make three blocks reversing colors.

assemble the throw pillow

1. Sew a 1½×11½" solid yellow border strip to the top and bottom edges of the Mariner's Compass block with muslin B pieces. Then add a 1½" muslin square to each end of the remaining 1½×11½"solid yellow border strips. Attach borders to side edges of block to make one throw pillow top.

2. Sew a 1½×11½" muslin border strip to the top and bottom edges of a Mariner's Compass block with solid yellow B pieces. Attach a solid yellow 1½" square to each end of the remaining 1½×11½" muslin border strips. Sew the borders to the side edges of the block to make a second throw pillow top.

3. With right sides together, place each throw pillow top atop a 13½" solid yellow square. Stitch the layers together on all sides, leaving an opening for turning. Turn each throw pillow cover right side out; press. Insert a 12" square

pillow form in each throw pillow cover. Whipstitch the openings closed.

assemble the bed-size pillow

1. Sew together the two remaining blocks to make a block rectangle.

2. Sew a 3×22½" muslin border strip to the top edge and one to the bottom edge of the block rectangle. Then add a 3" solid yellow square to each end of the 3×11½" muslin border strips. Add one of these strips to each side edge of the block rectangle.

3. Sew a 2×27½" solid yellow border strip to the top edge and bottom edge of the block rectangle.

4. Press a 1"-deep hem in one long edge of each 19½×16" solid yellow rectangle; stitch. Overlap the hemmed edges until the two rectangles together measure 19½×27½" for the pillow back.

5. Layer the pillow top and back with right sides together. Sew ¼" around all four sides. Turn the pillow cover right side out and press. Insert the standard bed pillow.

To complete the bedroom decor, make coordinating pillows—two small throw pillows and one bed-size pillow.

dolley madison's star

This traditional pattern is also known as "Santa Fe" and "President's Block." No matter what you call it, it's sure to land on your list of favorites once you piece it into a charming quilt.

materials

$2\frac{5}{8}$ yards of solid yellow for star blocks
    and binding
$4\frac{1}{2}$ yards of muslin for star blocks and sashing
5 yards of backing fabric
84" square of quilt batting

Finished quilt: 78" square
Finished block: 18" square

Quantities specified are for 44/45"-wide 100% cotton fabrics. All measurements include a $\frac{1}{4}$" seam allowance unless otherwise stated.

cut the fabrics

To make the best use of your fabrics, cut the pieces in the order that follows. There are no pattern pieces; the letter designations are for placement only.

If desired, increase the length of the sashing strips when cutting to allow for possible sewing differences. For this project, the sashing strips are cut the length of the fabric (parallel to the selvage).

From solid yellow, cut:
- 96–3" squares, cutting each in half diagonally for a total of 192 triangles for Position A
- 128–3" squares, cutting each in half diagonally for a total of 256 triangles for Position B

here's a tip
To thread a needle easily, moisten the needle eye instead of the thread. The capillary attraction of the saliva draws the thread right into the needle eye.

- *5–2½×42" strips for strip sets*
- *8–2½×42" binding strips*

From muslin, cut:

- *3–2½×78½" sashing strips*
- *4–2½×42" strips for strip sets*
- *12–2½×18½" sashing strips*
- *64–6½" squares for star blocks*
- *96–3" squares, cutting each in half diagonally for a total of 192 triangles for Position A*
- *64–3" squares, cutting each in half diagonally for a total of 128 triangles for Position B*
- *32–5⅛" squares, cutting each in half diagonally for a total of 64 triangles for Position C*

assemble the nine-patch units

1. Aligning long edges, sew two 2½×42" solid yellow strips to a 2½×42" muslin strip to make a Strip Set A (see Diagram 1). Press the seam allowances toward the solid yellow strips. Repeat to make a second Strip Set A. Cut the strip sets into thirty-two 2½"-wide segments.

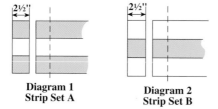

Diagram 1
Strip Set A

Diagram 2
Strip Set B

2. Aligning long edges, sew two 2½×42" muslin strips to a 2½×42" solid yellow strip to make a Strip Set B (see Diagram 2). Press the seam allowances toward the solid yellow strip. Cut the strip set into sixteen 2½"-wide segments.

3. Sew together two Strip Set A segments and one Strip Set B segment to make a Nine-Patch unit (see Diagram 3). Press the seam allowances toward the center segment. The Nine-Patch unit should

Diagram 3

measure 6½" square, including the seam allowances. Repeat to make a total of 16 Nine-Patch units.

assemble the star point units

1. Join one solid yellow A triangle and one muslin A triangle to make a triangle-square (see Diagram 4). Press seam allowance toward the solid yellow triangle. The pieced triangle-square should measure 2⅝" square, including the seam allowances. Repeat to make a total of 192 triangle-squares.

2. Referring to Diagram 5 for placement, lay out a triangle-square and two muslin B triangles. Join the pieces to make a Triangle Unit 1. Press the seam allowances toward the triangle-square. Repeat to make a total of 64 of Triangle Unit 1.

3. Referring to Diagram 6, lay out a triangle-square and two solid yellow B triangles. Join the pieces to make a Triangle Unit 2. Press the seam allowances toward the solid yellow triangles. Repeat to make a total of 128 of Triangle Unit 2.

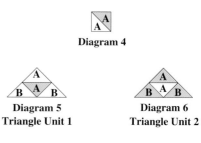

Diagram 4

Diagram 5
Triangle Unit 1

Diagram 6
Triangle Unit 2

4. Referring to Diagram 7, lay out one Triangle Unit 1, two of Triangle Unit 2, and a muslin C triangle. Sew together pieces in pairs. Press seam allowances in opposite directions. Then join pairs to make a star point unit. The pieced star point unit should measure 6½" square, including seam allowances. Repeat to make a total of 64 star point units.

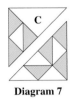

Diagram 7

assemble the dolley madison's star blocks

1. Referring to Diagram 8, lay out four star point units, four 6½" muslin squares, and one Nine-Patch unit in three horizontal rows.

2. Sew together the pieces in each row. Press the seam allowances toward the muslin squares or the Nine-Patch unit. Then join the rows to make a Dolley Madison's Star block. Press the seam allowances in one direction. The pieced block should measure 18½" square, including the seam allowances.

3. Repeat Steps 1 and 2 to make a total of 16 Dolley Madison's Star blocks.

assemble the quilt top

1. Referring to the photograph, *above*, lay out four Dolley Madison's Star blocks and three 2½×18½" muslin sashing strips in each of four horizontal rows. Sew together the blocks and sashing strips in each row. Press the seam allowances toward the sashing strips.

2. Lay out the rows and the 2½×78½" muslin sashing strips, alternating positions; join to complete the quilt top. Press seam allowances toward the sashing strips.

Diagram 8

complete the quilt

Layer the quilt top, batting, and backing according to the instructions in Quilter's Primer starting on *page 179*. Quilt as desired. This antique quilt is hand-quilted in a 1" diagonal grid that changes direction several times within the quilt. Use the 2½×42" solid yellow strips to bind the quilt according to the instructions in Quilter's Primer.

here's a tip
A loop knot can be substituted for a backstitch to secure pieces at each seam allowance intersection. The knot or backstitch gives the intersection strength.

fleur-de-lis quilt

This dramatic quilt was purchased at an auction in the 1960s for $12. While it came without any history, the vivid green indicates it was probably made in the 1870s or '80s. It has the unusual configuration of 12 full blocks and four half blocks.

 **pattern sheet**

materials

5¼ yards of solid green for appliqués

7 yards of solid ecru for appliqué foundations, borders, and binding

Freezer paper

81×91" of quilt batting

5⅛ yards of backing fabric

Light-color fabric marker

Finished quilt: 75×84"

Finished block: 18" square

Quantities specified are for 44/45"-wide 100% cotton fabrics. All measurements include a ¼" seam allowance unless otherwise stated.

designer notes

The appliquéd fleur-de-lis motif in the antique quilt in the photograph, *opposite*, was created with multiple pieces. To make it easier to position, this re-creation uses a one-piece fleur-de-lis.

These instructions are for needle-turn appliqué, an effective method for appliquéing small areas like those on this quilt. For best results, use small sharp scissors for snipping the tiny inner areas of both paper and fabric.

cut the fabrics

To make the best use of your fabrics, cut the pieces in the order that follows. To make a template of the Leaf Pattern, found on the Pattern Sheet, follow the instructions in Quilter's Primer, which begins on *page 179*. The border strips are

cut the length of the fabric (parallel to the selvage). If desired, increase length of these strips when cutting to allow for sewing differences.

From solid green, cut:
- *12−18½" squares for fleur-de-lis appliqués*
- *4−9½×18½" rectangles for fleur-de-lis appliqués*
- *1−18×42" rectangle, cutting it into ⅞"-wide bias strips for vine appliqué (see Cutting Bias Strips in the Quilter's Primer for instructions)*
- *275 of Leaf Pattern (Pattern Sheet)*

From solid ecru, cut:
- *2−6½×63½" border strips*
- *2−6½×84½" border strips*
- *12−20½" squares for appliqué foundations (trim the squares to 18½" after completing the appliqué)*
- *4−10½×20½" rectangles for appliqué foundations*
- *9−2½×42" binding strips*

cutting bias strips

Use a large acrylic triangle to square up the left edge of the 18×42" rectangle and to draw 45°-angle lines, ⅞" apart (see Bias Strip Diagram). Cut on the drawn lines to make bias strips. Handle the edges carefully to avoid distorting the bias. Cut enough ⅞"-wide strips to piece a 360"-long strip. Sew the bias strips together end to end.

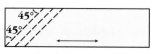

Bias Strip Diagram

prepare the fabrics

1. Fold one 18½" solid green square in half horizontally, making a rectangle (see Diagram 1). Fold the rectangle in half, making a 9¼" square. Then fold the square in half diagonally, bringing together the folded edges. Press the folded edges well to create precise placement lines. Repeat with the remaining green squares and the 20½" solid ecru squares.

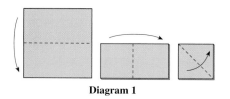

Diagram 1

2. Referring to Diagram 2, fold one 9½×18½" solid green rectangle in half, making a 9½×9¼" rectangle. Then fold the rectangle diagonally, leaving a ¼" seam allowance at the bottom; press well. Repeat with remaining green rectangles and the 10½×20½" solid ecru rectangles.

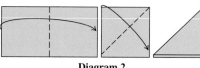

Diagram 2

prepare the templates

1. Cut the freezer paper into fourteen 18" squares. Fold each square, shiny side in, in the same manner as described in Steps 1 and 2 of Prepare the Fabrics, sharply creasing each fold. Staple the folds together in a corner to keep them stable.

2. Position the Fleur-de-Lis Pattern, found on the Pattern Sheet, on a folded freezer paper square as indicated. Tape or glue the pattern securely to the folded freezer paper.

3. Strategically pin or staple the layers to keep them from moving while cutting. Cut out the design carefully, including the inside open spaces.

4. Repeat with the remaining freezer-paper squares to make a total of 14 fleur-de-lis freezer-paper templates.

appliqué the blocks

1. Unfold one 18½" solid green square and one 20½" solid ecru square. Place the solid green square atop the solid ecru square with the right sides of both squares facing up. Carefully align the creases. Pin the squares together along the vertical and horizontal creases.

2. Carefully unfold one fleur-de-lis freezer-paper template. Position the freezer paper on the solid green square, matching the diagonal creases on the template to those on the fabric. Using a dry iron on cotton setting, press the freezer paper to the right side of green fabric. Trace the outline of the pattern with a light-color fabric marker. These marks must be visible throughout the appliqué process. Be sure that every part of the design has been traced; then remove the freezer paper. Baste inside each fleur-de-lis shape.

3. Cut the appliqué design a small portion at a time (2" to 3"), cutting a scant ⅛" away from the drawn lines; the lines serve as turn-under guides. Appliqué with small blind stitches, turning the edges under with your needle as you

here's a tip

When stitching a label on a quilt, affix it to the quilt backing before you quilt the project, then quilt through the label. This way you can be certain the quilt and label won't be parted.

work. To turn tight inside curves, clip the seam allowance up to the turn-under line. When appliquéing is complete, trim the solid ecru foundation to measure 18½" square, including seam allowances, centering the solid green appliqué.

4. Repeat Steps 1 through 3 to appliqué a total of 12 blocks.

5. Unfold one 9½×18½" solid green rectangle and one 10½×20½" solid ecru rectangle. Pin the solid green rectangle atop the solid ecru rectangle with creases aligned. Cut a fleur-de-lis freezer-paper template in half along the vertical fold line.

6. Position the half template on the solid green rectangle, matching diagonal creases and leaving a ¼" seam allowance at the bottom (see Diagram 3). Trace the template and appliqué design as before. Trim the top and side edges of the appliquéd half block to measure 9½×18½", including the seam allowances.

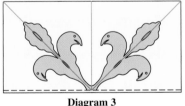

Diagram 3

7. Repeat Steps 5 and 6 to appliqué a total of four half blocks.

assemble the quilt center

Lay out the appliquéd blocks and half blocks in four rows. Sew together the pieces in each row. Press the seam allowances in one direction in each row, alternating the direction with each row. Then join the rows. Press seam allowances in one direction to make quilt center. The pieced quilt center should measure 63½×72½", including seam allowances.

assemble the borders

1. Sew one 6½×63½" solid ecru border strip to the top and bottom edges of the pieced quilt center. Press seam allowances toward the border.

2. Join one 6½×84½" solid ecru border strip to each side edge of the pieced quilt center to complete the quilt top. Press the seam allowances toward the borders.

appliqué the borders

1. Prepare the solid green Leaf Pattern pieces and vine bias strips by pressing under ³⁄₁₆" seam allowances.

2. Referring to the photograph on *page 155*, arrange the vine and leaves on the borders, spacing the leaves 1¾" to 2" apart. Baste the pieces in place.

3. Using thread that matches the solid green fabric, appliqué the vine and leaves to the borders.

complete the quilt

Layer the quilt top, batting, and backing according to the instructions in Quilter's Primer, beginning on *page 179*. Quilt as desired. The antique quilt pictured on *page 155* is hand-quilted in-the-ditch around all the appliqués. Echo quilting appears between the branches of each appliqué. The center is filled with diagonal lines. Use the nine 2½×42" solid ecru strips to bind the quilt according to the instructions in Quilter's Primer.

pinwheel quilt

Pieced pinwheel squares alternate with plain squares to create crossed rows of color. The wide solid yellow border enhances the quilt.

materials

5¾ yards of muslin for setting squares and patchwork

2⅞ yards of solid yellow fabric for borders

2 yards of yellow print fabric for patchwork

⅞ yard of binding fabric

5¾ yards of backing fabric

90×108" precut quilt batting

Finished quilt: 81¼×100¾"

Finished block: 9¾" square

Quantities specified are for 44/45"-wide 100% cotton fabrics. All measurements include a ¼" seam allowance unless otherwise stated.

instructions

The Pinwheel block is assembled like a nine-patch: five pieced Pinwheel squares alternating with four plain squares. The finished blocks are joined in an alternate straight set and framed with a wide border.

cutting the fabrics

From muslin, cut:

- *1–42×83" rectangle (from this piece, cut 31–10¼" setting squares)*
- *1–42×45" rectangle (from this piece, cut 128 squares for the Pinwheel blocks, each 3¾" square)*
- *1–42×72" rectangle (from this piece, cut 8–17" squares and 3–8×17" rectangles for the triangle-squares)*

here's a tip

To avoid confusion when you're piecing, keep like units pinned together with a label or in a labeled storage bag or container. This prevents inadvertently grabbing the wrong piece.

From yellow print fabric, cut:

- *8—17" squares*
- *3—8×17" rectangles*

From solid yellow fabric, cut:

- *2—7×85" strips*
- *2—7×103" strips*

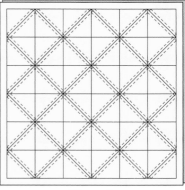

Diagram 1

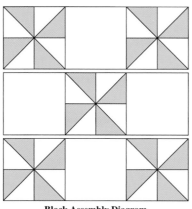

Block Assembly Diagram

assemble the triangle-squares

1. On each 17" square of muslin, mark a 6×6 grid of 2½" squares as shown in Diagram 1. Draw diagonal lines through the squares as shown. Layer each muslin square, marked side up, atop one matching 17" square of yellow print fabric.

2. For traditional piecing, cut the triangles apart on the marked lines. For hand piecing, use a fabric pencil and a gridded ruler to mark ¼" seam allowances on each triangle.

3. For quick piecing, stitch the grid. Each grid makes 72 triangle-squares.

4. Repeat the procedure with the 8×17" pieces, marking a 2×6 grid of 2½" squares on each muslin piece as shown in Diagram 2. Each of these grids produces 24 triangle-squares.

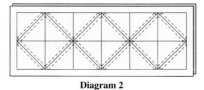

Diagram 2

5. Using either piecing method, make 640 triangle-squares. Press the seam allowances toward the yellow fabric. Discard any damaged or distorted triangle-squares.

here's a tip

If you have trouble with your thread not pulling off the spool properly, check how the spool is situated on the machine's spool pin. If the thread is pulling out from the underside of the spool, turn the spool over so the thread feeds off over the top of the spool (or vice versa). Sometimes this changes the thread tension enough to make a difference in the stitch quality.

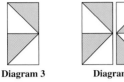

Diagram 3   **Diagram 4**

assemble the pinwheel blocks

1. Join all the triangle-squares in pairs, positioning the yellow print fabric as shown in Diagram 3. Press all the joining seam allowances in the same direction.

2. Sew two pairs of triangle-squares together to create one Pinwheel square, turning one of the pairs upside down to position the fabrics as shown in Diagram 4. Make 160 Pinwheel squares.

3. Each Pinwheel block is made from five Pinwheel squares and four 3¾" muslin squares. Refer to the Block Assembly Diagram, *opposite*, and join the squares in three rows.

4. Press the joining seam allowances toward the muslin squares; then assemble the rows as shown to complete the block.

5. Repeat Steps 3 to 4 to make a total of 32 Pinwheel blocks.

assembling the quilt top

This quilt is assembled in nine horizontal rows of seven blocks each.

Sew the blocks into rows, alternating Pinwheel blocks and plain muslin blocks. Make five rows with pieced blocks at both ends and four rows with muslin blocks at both ends. Press seam allowances toward the plain blocks.

Join rows so the pieced and plain blocks alternate. The first and last rows start with pieced blocks so that all four corners of the quilt top have a Pinwheel block.

assembling the borders

Review instructions for mitering border corners in Quilter's Primer, beginning on *page 179*. Following these instructions, sew the longer border strips to the quilt sides; sew the remaining border strips to the top and bottom edges. Miter corners; trim excess border fabric from the seam allowances.

complete the quilt

Layer the quilt top, batting, and backing according to the instructions in Quilter's Primer. Quilt as desired. The quilt sample has an X quilted across each triangle-square. The same four-X design is repeated in the plain squares of each Pinwheel block. A feathered wreath fills the plain blocks.

See Quilter's Primer for tips on binding. Use the ⅞ yard of binding fabric to make approximately 370" straight-grain binding.

here's a tip
When it's time to change threads, cut the thread at the spool and pull the remaining thread out through the needle. This prevents thread pieces from breaking off in the tension discs or getting stuck inside your machine.

lincoln quilt

Making a patchwork checkerboard, or any pattern with parallelograms, is a delight with the strip technique used to make this pink-and-white work of art.

Although the Lincoln Quilt, *opposite,* appears intricate, the quilt top comprises components that are ideal for quick-piecing.

The quick-piecing method used to create this quilt involves cutting fabric into strips with a rotary cutter, sewing together alternate colors of the strips in sets, and assembling the sets into a checkerboard pattern. Although the squares for this quilt are very small–the finished size of each one is ⅝"–the same technique is used for making any patchwork based on squares and rectangles. Quilt instructions begin on *page 164.*

The basic construction method for many patchwork designs based on squares and rectangles is to stitch the squares into horizontal rows and then join the rows together to piece the design. When the squares occur in a regular sequence, they can be quickly pieced into rows on the sewing machine without marking and cutting each individual square.

1. Measure the finished size of the square; add ½" to this measurement to allow for ¼" seam allowances on all sides.

For the Lincoln Quilt, *opposite,* the center portion of the block is a rectangle made of many small squares. The finished squares are ⅝" so the strip width measurement with seam allowances is 1⅛".

Isolate the first row of the design. Count the number of times each fabric

is used in the row. For the sample quilt, the first row is made of seven dark pink squares and six white squares.

The second row of the design is made of seven white squares and six dark pink squares. These two rows repeat to make the rectangle.

Use a rotary cutter and ruler to cut 13 strips, each 1⅛" wide and approximately 45" long, from both the dark pink and white fabrics.

You can mark each strip, then cut the strips with scissors if you do not have a rotary cutter and ruler, but cutting the strips with a rotary cutter and ruler is faster and more accurate. (See Photo A, *page 164.*)

2. Sew the strips into strip sets using ¼" seam allowances. Sew the strips in the same sequence as they occur in the design row.

Make the Strip Set 1 (*page 165,* Diagram 1) for the first row by alternating seven dark pink strips with six white strips. Press seam allowances all in one direction.

Make the Strip Set 2 (*page 165,* Diagram 1)for the second row by alternating seven white strips with six dark pink strips. Press the seam allowances in the opposite direction from the way Strip Set 1 was pressed.

Layer the strip sets right sides together with the seam allowances

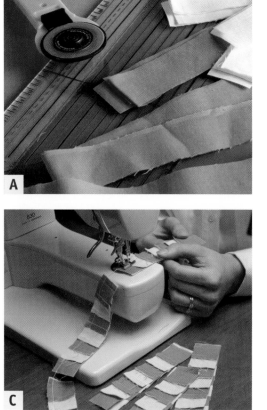

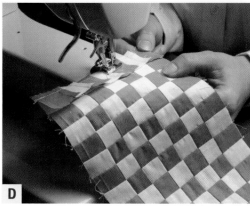

going in opposite directions. Using a ruler and rotary cutter, cut the strip sets into segments the same width that the strips were cut. (Cut 38 segments, each 1⅛" wide for the quilt shown.) Check after cutting every three or four strips to verify the cuts are at right angles to the strips. Trim the edge to square it, if necessary, before cutting more strips. (See Photo B, *above.*)

3. Pick a pair of segments (each pair has a Strip Set 1 segment and a Strip Set 2 segment with right sides facing). Stitch the pairs together, matching the squares at each intersection. Insert pins so they are perpendicular to the seam lines to align the squares in each segment.

Without clipping the thread, stitch a second pair of segments. Continue to stitch additional pairs. Chain the segments together with a short length of thread. Chain-piecing the pairs is much faster than stopping and starting after each pair. (See Photo C.)

4. Join the pairs of segments to other pairs and repeat until the block is the needed size. For the sample quilt, join six pairs of segments then add a single Strip Set 1 segment to complete the center rectangle. (See Photo D.)

Quantities specified are for 44/45"-wide 100% cotton fabrics. All measurements include a ¼" seam allowance unless otherwise stated.

materials

7 yards of white fabric

4 yards of dark pink fabric

1 yard of pink fabric

4½ yards backing fabric

Quilt batting

Plastic or cardboard for templates

Finished quilt: 72¾×72¾"

Finished block: 14⅛"

instructions

The instructions for this quilt are written for quick-piecing on the sewing machine. Refer to the diagrams and instructions, on *page 162* and *opposite*, for tips on quick-piecing squares. Stitch using ¼" seams.

Trace and make templates for the patterns, *page 167*. Patterns are finished size; add ¼" seam allowances when cutting the pieces from the fabric. Measurements for the sashing strips and strips for quick-piecing squares include seam allowances.

to cut the pieces

Cut the strips for this quilt using a rotary cutter, heavy plastic ruler, and a cutting mat or mark the pieces with a ruler and cut them with scissors.

From white fabric, cut:

40–4¾×14⅝" sashing strips

63–1⅛×45" quick-piecing strips

356 of Triangle B with the long side on the fabric grain (page 167)

292 of Square C (page 167)

64 of Square D (page 167)

128 of Triangle E with the long side on the fabric grain (page 167)

From dark pink fabric, cut:

59–quick-piecing strips, each 1⅛×45"

356–diamonds from Template A (page 167)

9 yards of 2½"-wide strips for the binding

From pink fabric, cut:

356 of Diamond A (page 167)

to piece the blocks:

1. Refer to the quick-piecing squares instructions. Make five each of Strip Set 1 and Strip Set 2 as described in the instructions. Cut a total of 176 pairs of segments. Cut 16 additional segments of Strip Set 2.

Referring to the instructions and Diagram 1, *below,* make 16 rectangular center sections for the blocks.

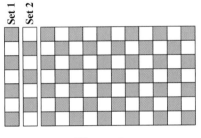

Diagram 1

Referring to Diagram 2, *below,* use Strip Set 1 segments and Strip Set 2 segments to piece 32 rectangles. Add D squares to the ends of the rectangles.

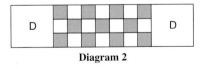

Diagram 2

Referring to Diagram 3, *below,* make two of Strip Set 3 by sewing together five dark pink strips and four white strips. Cut into a total of 64 segments.

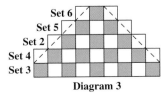

Diagram 3

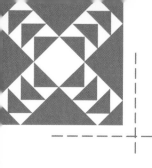

Make two of Strip Set 4 by sewing together five white strips and four dark pink strips. Cut into a total of 64 segments.

Make two of Strip Set 5 by sewing together three white strips and two dark pink strips. Cut into a total of 64 segments.

Make two of Strip Set 6 by sewing together two white strips and one dark pink strip. Cut into a total of 64 segments.

Stitch together the strip segments as shown in Diagram 3; trim off excess squares along seams. Sew an E triangle onto both sides. Make a total of 64 Diagram 3 units.

Referring to Diagram 4, *below*, piece 64 partial star blocks for the block corners.

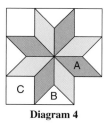

Diagram 4

To make one block, refer to Diagram 5, *opposite*. Sew a Diagram 2 unit to top and bottom sides of a Diagram 1 unit. Add Diagram 3 units to the four sides of the center square. Set in Diagram 4 units at the four corners.

assemble the quilt top

Make 16 Lincoln Quilt blocks.

Referring to Diagram 4, *above*, piece 25 additional Star blocks for outer edges,

completing blocks by joining a C square in the open corner to make full squares.

Referring to quilt on *page 163*, sew the blocks into four rows with four blocks in each row, joining sashing strips between the blocks and at the beginning and end of the rows.

Sew five sashing strip rows by sewing together four sashing strips with Star blocks between the strips and at the beginning and end of the rows.

Sew together the block rows and sashing strip rows.

complete the quilt

To piece the quilt back, cut fabric into two equal lengths. Cut one length in half lengthwise. Sew one narrow panel to each side of the wide panel. Match the selvages; use a ½" seam. Trim the seams to ¼"; press to one side.

Trace the quilting design, *opposite*, and transfer the design to the inside sashing strips, drawing three leaves on each strip. Mark horizontal lines in outside sashing strips.

Layer the back, batting, and pieced top. Baste layers together; quilt.

Splice the binding strips together at 45° angles. Trim, fold in half lengthwise with wrong sides together, and press.

When quilting is complete, trim away excess batting and backing so all edges are even with the quilt top. Sew the binding to the right side of the quilt, raw edges together. Turn the folded edge to the back; hand-stitch in place.

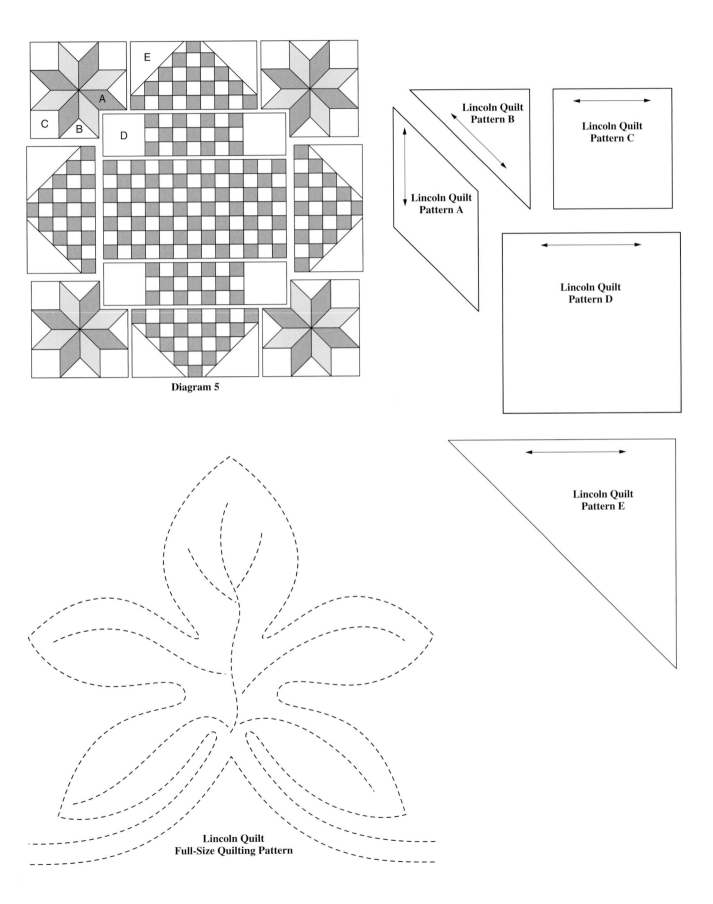

Diagram 5

Lincoln Quilt
Pattern B

Lincoln Quilt
Pattern C

Lincoln Quilt
Pattern A

Lincoln Quilt
Pattern D

Lincoln Quilt
Pattern E

Lincoln Quilt
Full-Size Quilting Pattern

sweet inspiration quilt

Using a contrasting two-color scheme—pink and white—this quilt displays an inspirational combination of triangles and squares. Small nine-patch checkerboards highlight the corners.

materials

1½ yards of muslin for blocks,
borders, and binding
1¼ yards of pink print for blocks and borders
1¼ yards of backing fabric
44" square of quilt batting

Finished quilt: 38" square
Finished block: 8" square

Quantities specified are for 44/45"-wide 100% cotton fabrics. All measurements include a ¼" seam allowance unless otherwise stated.

cut the fabrics

To make the best use of your fabrics, cut the pieces in the order that follows. For this project, the border strips are cut lengthwise (parallel to the selvage). This listing includes the mathematically correct border strip lengths. If desired, increase the length of the strips now to allow for sewing differences later. Trim the borders to the correct size after sewing them to the quilt top.

From muslin, cut:
• *4–2×42" strips for binding strips*
• *8–1½×32½" strips for border strips*
• *16–1½" squares for Position D*
• *16–2½" squares for Position A*
• *8–6⅞" squares, cutting each in half diagonally for a total of 16 triangles for Position C*
• *48–2⅞" squares, cutting each in half diagonally for a total of 96 triangles for Position B*

From pink print, cut:
• *4–1½×32½" strips for borders*
• *20–1½" squares for Position D*
• *8–6⅞" squares, cutting each in half diagonally for a total of 16 triangles for Position C*
• *48–2⅞" squares, cutting each in half diagonally for a total of 96 triangles for Position B*

assemble the blocks

1. For one block gather one muslin A square, six muslin B triangles, six pink print B triangles, one muslin C triangle, and one pink print C triangle.

2. With right sides together and long edges aligned, sew together the pink print C triangle and the muslin C triangle (see Diagram 1) to make a large triangle–square. Press the seam allowances toward the pink triangle.

Diagram 1 (triangle-square)

The pieced large triangle–square should measure 6½" square, including seam allowances.

3. With right sides together and long edges aligned, sew together one pink print B triangle and one muslin B triangle to make a small triangle–square. Press the seam allowance toward the pink triangle. The pieced small

triangle-square should measure
2½" square, including the seam
allowances. Repeat for a total of six
small triangle-squares.

4. Referring to Diagram 2 for placement,
sew together two rows of three small
triangle-squares. Press the seam
allowances in one direction.

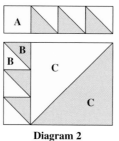

Diagram 2
Make 16 blocks

Sew one row to the left-hand side of
the large triangle-square. Press the seam
allowance toward the large triangle-
square. To the left-hand end of the
remaining row, join the muslin A
square. Press the seam allowance
toward the muslin square. Sew this row
to the top of the large triangle-square.
Press the seam allowance toward the
large triangle-square. The pieced block
should measure 8½" square, including
the seam allowances.

5. Repeat Steps 1 through 4 for a total of
16 Sweet Inspiration blocks.

assemble the quilt top

Referring to the photograph, *left,* lay
out the blocks in four rows of four
blocks each. In this quilt, the
directions of the blocks are alternated
to create additional interest.

Sew together the blocks in each
row. Press the seam allowances in
one direction, alternating the
direction with each row. Then join
the rows. Press the seam
allowances in one direction. The
pieced quilt top should
measure 32½" square, including
the seam allowances.

assemble the borders

1. Referring to Diagram 3, lay out four muslin D squares and five pink print D squares in three rows of three squares

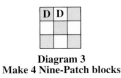

Diagram 3
Make 4 Nine-Patch blocks

each, alternating colors. Sew together the squares in each row. Press the seam allowances toward the pink squares. Join the rows to make a Nine-Patch corner block. Press the seam allowances in one direction. The pieced Nine-Patch corner block should measure 3½" square, including the seam allowances.

2. Repeat Step 1 to make a total of four Nine-Patch corner blocks.

3. With right sides together and long raw edges aligned, sew one 1½×32½" muslin strip to each side of a 1½×32½" pink print strip. Press the seam allowances toward the pink strip. The pieced border strip set should measure 3½×32½", including seam allowances.

4. Repeat Step 3 to make a total of four border strip sets.

5. Sew one border strip set to the top edge of the pieced quilt top and one to the bottom edge. Press the seam allowances toward the borders. To each end of the remaining border strip sets, connect Nine-Patch corner blocks. Press the seam allowances toward the border strip set. Then join these border strip sets to each side of the pieced quilt top. Press the seam allowances toward the border.

complete the quilt

Layer the quilt top, batting, and backing according to the instructions in Quilter's Primer beginning on *page 179*. The quilt sample was machine quilted in parallel rows to form checkerboards in the large areas. It is also machine quilted in-the-ditch on the border.

Finish the quilt following the binding instructions in Quilter's Primer.

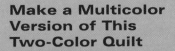

Make a Multicolor Version of This Two-Color Quilt

Amish quiltmakers choose striking color combinations. This wall hanging sample includes rich, vibrant colors that come together for a dramatic Amish-style finish. Wide border strips and single corner squares finish the project.

snowball

The Snowball quilt is a variation of the Robbing Peter to Pay Paul pattern created by alternating images of two contrasting fabrics. Together the blocks create the illusion of white stars on a pink background—or is it pink stars on white?

materials

5 yards of muslin or white fabric
4 yards of solid pink fabric
2¾ yards of backing fabric
90×108" precut quilt batting; template material
Rotary cutter, mat, and acrylic ruler

Finished quilt top: 88½" square
Finished block: 8" square

instructions

Eighty-one blocks in this quilt are assembled in a 9×9-block straight set framed by a three-strip border with pieced corners.

cut the fabrics

Refer to Quilter's Primer beginning on *page 179* for tips on making templates for patchwork. Make a Window Template for Pattern A on *page 175*. Make a template for the half-pattern as given and mark on folded fabric, or make a template for the complete shape so you can mark on a single layer of fabric. Mark both cutting and sewing lines for Pattern A.

From the pink fabric, cut:
• *1–13×86" piece for borders (from this piece, cut 4–3¼×79" strips for the middle border and 8–3¼" squares for the corners of the other two borders)*

here's a tip

Some quilters prefer to avoid clipping curved seams. Instead they use a longer stitch length and sew slowly, which helps ease the fabric layers together (the center notch is still necessary).

- *10–3⅝×29" strips (from these strips, cut 80–3⅝" squares–cutting each square in half diagonally to obtain 160 triangles)*
- *41 of Pattern A (page 175)*

From the muslin, cut:

- *1–25×42" piece for binding*
- *1–26×84" piece for borders (From this piece, cut 4–3¼×73" strips for the inner border and 4–3¼×84" strips for the outer border. From the scrap at the end of the shorter borders, cut 4–3¼" squares for the corners of the middle border.)*
- *21–3⅝×16" strips (from these strips, cut 82–3⅝" squares–cutting each square in half diagonally to obtain 164 triangles)*
- *40 of Pattern A (page 175)*

assemble the blocks

Throughout the construction of the blocks, press the seam allowances toward the darker fabric.

1. Stitch a pink triangle onto one diagonal edge of a white A piece. Add pink triangles to the three remaining diagonal edges to complete the block. Make 40 Snowball blocks in this manner.

2. Repeat, sewing four white triangles onto each pink A piece. Make 41 of these blocks.

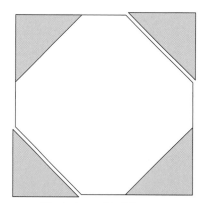

Block Assembly Diagram

assemble the quilt top

Join the blocks into nine horizontal rows of nine blocks each, alternating pink and white centers. Make five rows that have pink-center blocks at each end and four rows that have white-center blocks at each end.

Join the rows, alternating the block colors and matching seam lines carefully. The assembled quilt top should be approximately 72" square.

assemble the borders

1. Stitch a 3¼×73" white border strip onto the top edge of the quilt. Stitch a matching border strip to the bottom edge. Press the seam allowances toward the border strips; trim borders even with the sides of the quilt top.

2. Sew a 3¼" square of pink fabric to both ends of the remaining 73"-long border strips. Join these to the sides of the quilt top, matching the seam lines of the corner squares with the seam lines of the top and bottom borders. Adjust the corner square seams to make the side borders shorter or longer as necessary.

3. Stitch the middle border in the same manner, sewing pink strips at the top and bottom edges of the quilt top and then adding the side borders with white corner squares.

4. Use the 3¼×84" white strips for the outer border. Join pink squares to the side borders.

complete the quilt

Layer the quilt top, batting, and backing according to the instructions in Quilter's Primer beginning on *page 179*. Quilt as desired.

On the quilt pictured on *page 173* six different designs are quilted in the white octagons. One of these quilting designs is shown on Pattern A, *opposite*. Quilt the pink A octagons with a grid of 1" squares and outline quilt the triangles inside the seam lines. Quilt a cable of interlocked ovals over the combined width of the border strips.

For instructions on binding, see the Quilter's Primer. Make approximately 360" straight-grain binding.

here's a tip

Keep a TV tray in your sewing room and set it up when you need extra table space. It also comes in handy when you need a small ironing surface, such as when you're paper piecing or making Log Cabin blocks. Top the tray with a small pressing pad and stand it alongside your sewing machine so you can press as you go. Tuck the folded tray out of the way when not needed.

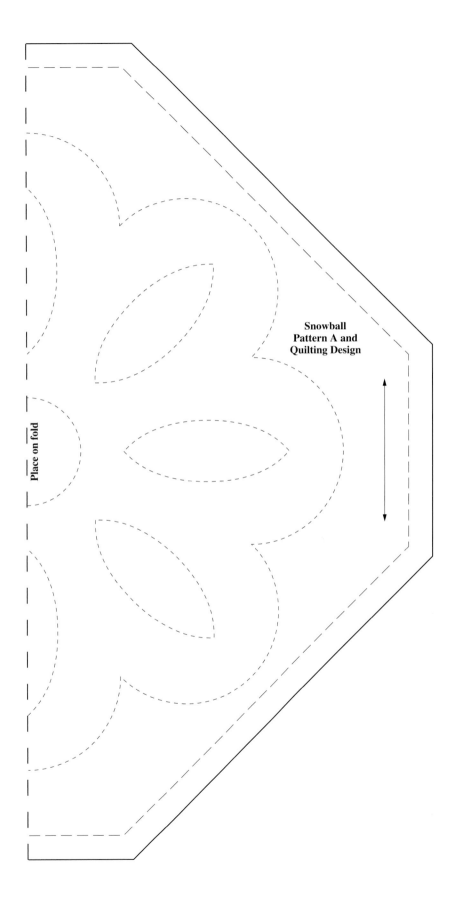

Place on fold

Snowball Pattern A and Quilting Design

hearts and gizzards quilt

Only two shapes... only two colors... who would guess you could create something so splendid? This traditional quilt block receives a pretty pastel coat of pink paired with fresh white.

materials

8¾ yards of white fabric
7¼ yards of pink fabric
3 yards of 90"-wide sheeting for backing fabric
90×108" precut quilt batting
Template material

Finished quilt top: 86¾×98"
Finished block: 11¼" square.

Quantities specified are for 44/45"-wide 100% cotton fabrics. All measurements include a ¼" seam allowance unless otherwise stated.

instructions

This quilt is a straight set consisting of 56 blocks sewn together in eight horizontal rows of seven blocks each. The quilt is bordered with 4"-wide strips of white fabric.

cut the fabrics

Refer to Quilter's Primer, beginning on *page 179* for tips on making templates for patchwork. Prepare a template for Pattern A, *page 178.*

From white fabric, cut:
- *2–4½×100" border strips*
- *2–4½×81" border strips*
- *1–33" square for binding*
- *112–6½" squares, cutting each in half diagonally for a total of 224 triangles*
- *448 of Pattern A (page 178)*

From pink fabric, cut:
- *112–6½-inch squares, cutting each in half diagonally for a total of 224 triangles*
- *448 of Pattern A (page 178)*

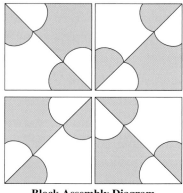

Block Assembly Diagram

assemble the blocks

The Hearts and Gizzards block consists of four identical squares. Each square is made by joining triangles of different colors, but each triangle is first appliquéd with two half-hearts of the opposite color. At the center of the block, the joined squares form a wheel of hearts in an interchange of pink and white.

1. Baste under the curved edge of two pink A pieces.

2. Referring to the Block Assembly Diagram, *above,* for placement, pin or baste the prepared A pieces on opposite corners of a white triangle, matching all raw edges.

3. Appliqué the curved edges of both A pieces on the white triangle. When appliquéing is complete, press lightly. Trim away the white fabric under the

here's a tip
If residue from basting spray or a glue stick builds up on your needle, wipe it off with rubbing alcohol.

appliquéd A pieces, leaving a ¼" seam allowance of pink fabric under the curved edge.

4. In this manner, make 224 white triangles and 224 pink triangles.

5. Stitch one white triangle and one pink triangle together to form a square as shown in the Block Assembly Diagram. Make 224 squares.

6. Join four squares to complete a block, positioning squares as shown in the Block Assembly Diagram for correct color placement. Make 56 blocks.

assemble the quilt top

1. Stitch seven blocks together in a row. Make eight rows of seven blocks each. Press the seam allowances to one side.

2. Matching seam lines carefully, join the rows to complete the quilt top. The assembled quilt top should measure approximately 78¾×90".

assemble the borders

Stitch a short border strip to top and bottom edges of the quilt top. Press seam allowances toward the borders; trim excess border fabric. Join side borders in the same manner.

complete the quilt

Layer the quilt top, batting, and backing according to the instructions in Quilter's Primer. Quilt as desired.

The quilt pictured on *page 177* has outline quilting inside each A piece and a shape resembling a fleur-de-lis quilted inside each triangle. A simple cable is quilted in the border strips.

For instructions on binding, see the Quilter's Primer. Make approximately 376 inches of binding.

here's a tip
Keep a bar of soap handy to use as a pincushion. Pins and needles can be struck through the paper wrapper. The soap helps the needles and pins slide easily into cotton fabrics.

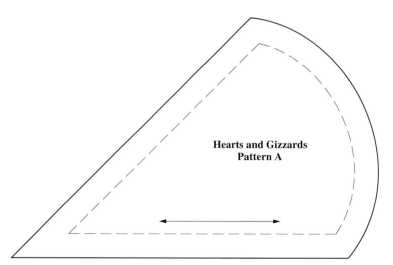

Hearts and Gizzards
Pattern A

quilter's primer

Before beginning any project, read through these general quilting instructions to ensure you'll properly cut and assemble your quilt. Accuracy in each step guarantees a successful quiltmaking experience.

tools

The following list includes basic supplies that you may need to make the projects found in this book. If a project requires a special tool or piece of equipment, it will be listed in that project's materials list.

- **Acrylic ruler:** Choose a ruler of thick, clear plastic that can be used with a rotary cutter. Many sizes are available.
- **Pencils and other marking tools:** Marks made with special quilt markers are easy to remove after sewing and quilting.
- **Rotary cutter and mat:** A rotary cutter's round, sharp blade can cut through several layers of fabric at one time. It cuts strips, squares, triangles, and diamonds more quickly, efficiently, and accurately than scissors. A rotary cutter should always be used with a self-healing mat designed specifically for it. In addition to protecting the table, the mat helps keep the fabric from shifting while you cut.
- **Scissors:** You'll need one pair to cut curved and irregularly shaped fabric pieces and another to cut paper and plastic.
- **Template plastic:** This slightly frosted plastic comes in thin, sturdy sheets.

piecing

- **Iron and ironing board**
- **Sewing machine:** Any machine with well-adjusted tension will produce pucker-free patchwork seams.
- **Sewing thread:** Use 100-percent-cotton or cotton-covered polyester sewing thread.

hand quilting

- **Frame or hoop:** You'll get smaller, tighter stitches if you stretch your quilt for stitching. A frame supports the quilt's weight, ensures even tension, and frees both hands for quilting. Hoops are more portable and less expensive. Quilting hoops are deeper than embroidery hoops to handle the thickness of quilt layers.
- **Quilting needles:** A "between" or quilting needle is a short needle with a small eye. Common sizes are 8, 9, and 10; size 8 is best for beginners.
- **Quilting thread:** Choose a 100-percent-cotton quilting thread.
- **Thimble:** This finger cover relieves the pressure required to push a needle through several layers of fabric and batting.

machine quilting

- **Darning foot:** A darning, or hopper, foot is used for free-motion stitching. You may find it in your sewing machine's accessory kit. If not, have the machine brand and model available when you go to purchase one.
- **Quilting thread:** Choose from 100-percent-cotton, cotton-covered polyester, or very fine nylon quilting thread.

quilter's primer continued

- **Safety pins:** These clasps hold the layers together during quilting.
- **Table or other large work surface: Use a surface** that is level with your machine bed.
- **Walking foot:** This sewing machine accessory helps keep long, straight quilting lines smooth.

fabrics

We specify all quantities for 44/45"-wide, 100-percent-cotton fabrics unless otherwise noted. We allow for narrow widths and shrinkage by figuring yardage based on a 42" width, with additional yardage in length for minor errors. If the fabric you're working with measures less than 42" wide, you'll need more than the specified amount.

make the templates

For some quilts, you'll need to cut out the same shape up to 200 times. For accurate piecing later, the individual pieces should be identical to one another.

A template is a pattern made from an extra-sturdy material so you can trace around it many times without wearing away the edges. Acrylic templates for many common shapes are available at quilt shops. You can make your own templates by duplicating the patterns on our pattern sheets. Then you can transfer the patterns to fabric by tracing around the templates.

To make a template, we recommend using easy-to-cut template plastic, available at crafts supply stores. Lay the plastic over a printed pattern. Trace the pattern onto the plastic using a ruler and a permanent marker. This will ensure straight lines, accurate corners, and permanency.

For hand piecing and appliqué, make templates the exact size of the finished pieces, without seam allowances, by tracing the patterns' dashed lines. For machine piecing, make templates with ¼" seam allowances included.

For easy reference, mark each template with its letter designation, grain line, and block name. Verify a template's size by placing it over the printed pattern. To check the templates' accuracy, make a test block before cutting the pieces for an entire quilt.

plan for cutting

All dimensions given in cutting instructions include a ¼" seam allowance. Patchwork patterns are full-size, include a ¼" seam allowance, and show both the seam (dashed) and cutting (solid) lines. Appliqué patterns do not include a seam allowance.

Always consider the fabric grain before cutting fabric pieces. The arrow on a pattern piece indicates which direction the fabric grain should run. One or more straight sides of the fabric piece should follow the fabric's lengthwise or crosswise grain. The lengthwise grain, parallel to the selvage (the tightly finished edge), has the least amount of stretch. Crosswise grain, perpendicular to the selvage, has a little more give. The edge of any fabric piece that will be on the outside of a block should be cut on the lengthwise grain.

Strips for meandering vines and other curved appliqué pattern pieces should be cut on the bias (diagonally across the grain of a woven fabric), which runs at a 45° angle to the selvage and has the most give or stretch.

trace the templates

To mark on fabric, use a pencil, white dressmaker's pencil, chalk, or a special quilt marker that makes a thin, accurate line. Do not use a ballpoint or ink pen that may bleed if washed. Test all marking tools on a fabric scrap before using them.

To trace pieces that will be used for hand piecing or appliqué, place templates facedown on the wrong side of the fabric; position the tracings at least ½" apart (see Diagram 1).

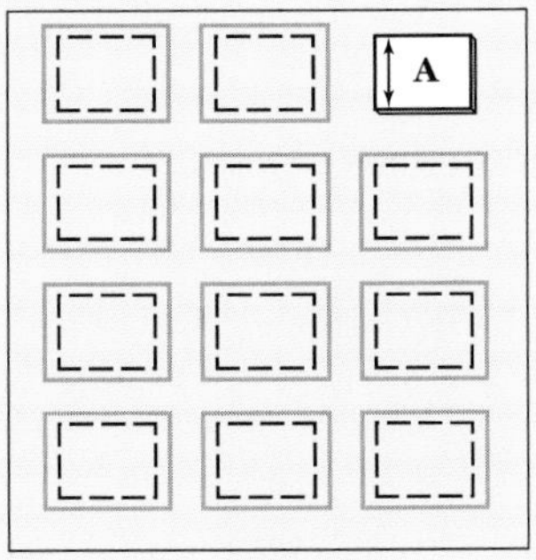

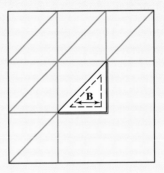

Diagram 1

The lines traced on the fabric are the sewing lines. Mark a seam allowance (cutting lines) around each piece and cut out. Or, when cutting out the pieces, estimate a seam allowance by eye. For hand piecing, add a ¼" seam allowance; for hand appliqué, add a ³⁄₁₆" seam allowance.

Templates used to make pieces for machine piecing have seam allowances included so you can use common lines for

efficient cutting. To trace, place the templates facedown on the wrong side of the fabric; position them without space in between (see Diagram 2). Cut out precisely on the drawn (cutting) lines.

Diagram 2

appliqué

In some quilt patterns, especially those with rounded shapes, one layer of fabric is appliquéd, or sewn atop another. The most-used methods of appliqué are as follows.

- **Traditional:** Trace the template on the right side of the fabric, then cut out ³⁄₁₆" beyond the traced line. Press the ³⁄₁₆" seam allowance to the wrong side along the traced line. Pin, then slip-stitch the shape atop the foundation fabric.

- **Fusible appliqué:** This method uses paper-backed fusing-adhesive material to permanently bond the appliqué shape to the foundation fabric. Depending on the pattern, you can trace the template (omitting seam allowances) onto the material's paper side before or after it is bonded to the appliqué fabric. After it's bonded, finish the edges with decorative hand or machine stitches.

cut the bias strips

Strips for curved appliqué pattern pieces and for binding curved edges should be cut on the bias (diagonally across the grain of a woven fabric), which runs at a 45° angle to the selvage and has the most stretch.

To cut bias strips, begin with a fabric square or rectangle. Use a large acrylic ruler to square the left edge and make a 45° angle cut (see Diagram 3). Cut the fabric on the drawn lines. Handle the edges carefully to avoid distorting the bias. Cut enough strips to total the length needed.

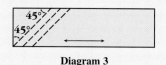

Diagram 3

cover the cording

Covered cording is made by sewing a bias-cut fabric strip around a length of cording. The width of the bias strip varies according to the diameter of the cording; refer to specific project instructions for measurements.

With the wrong side inside, fold under 1" at one end of the bias strip, then fold the strip in half lengthwise to make the cording cover. Insert the cording next to the folded edge, placing a cording end 1" from the cording cover folded end. Using a machine cording foot, sew through both fabric layers right next to the cording.

When attaching the cording to your project, begin stitching 1½" from the covered cording's folded end. Round the

corners slightly, making sure the corner curves match. As you stitch each corner, gently ease the covered cording into place (see Diagram 4).

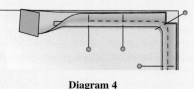

Diagram 4

After going around the entire edge of the project, cut the end of the cording so that it will fit snugly into the folded opening at the beginning (see Diagram 5).

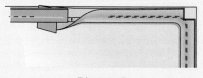

Diagram 5

The ends of the cording should abut inside the covering. Stitch the ends in place to secure (see Diagram 6).

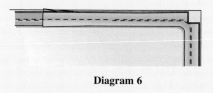

Diagram 6

complete the quilt

Cut and piece the backing fabric to measure at least 3" bigger on all sides than the quilt top. Press all seam allowances open. With wrong sides together, layer the quilt top and backing with the batting in between; baste. Quilt as desired.

The binding for most quilts is cut on the straight grain of the fabric. The cutting instructions specify the number of binding strips needed to finish the quilt with a French-fold, or double-layer, binding, which is the easiest type to apply and adds durability.

Join the strips with diagonal seams (see Diagram 7) to make one continuous binding strip. Trim the excess fabric, leaving 1/4" seam allowances. Press the seam allowances open. Then, with the wrong side inside, fold under 1" on one end of the binding strip (see Diagram 8); press. Fold the strip in half lengthwise, again with the wrong side inside (see Diagram 9); press.

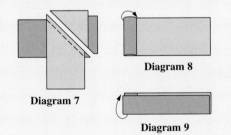

Diagram 8

Diagram 7

Diagram 9

Beginning at the center of one side, place the prepared binding strip against the right side of the quilt top, aligning the binding strip raw edges with the quilt top raw edge (see Diagram 10).

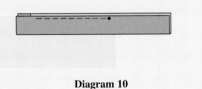

Diagram 10

Sew through all layers, stopping 1/4" from the corner. Backstitch, then clip the threads. Remove the quilt from under the sewing-machine presser foot.

Fold the binding strip upward (see Diagram 11), creating a diagonal fold, and

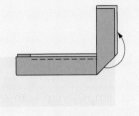

Diagram 11

finger-press.

Holding the diagonal fold in place with your finger, bring down the binding strip in line with the next edge, making a horizontal fold that aligns with the first

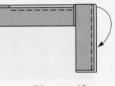

Diagram 12

edge of the quilt (see Diagram 12).

Start sewing again at the top of the horizontal fold, stitching through all layers. Sew around the quilt, turning each corner in the same manner.

When you return to the starting point, lap the binding strip inside the beginning fold (see Diagram 13).

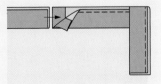

Diagram 13

quilter's primer continued

Finish sewing to the starting point (see Diagram 14).

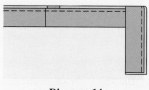

Diagram 14

Trim the batting and backing fabric even with the quilt top edges.

Turn the binding over the edge of the quilt to the back. Hand-stitch the binding to the backing, making sure to cover any machine stitching.

To make mitered corners on the back, hand-stitch the binding up to a corner; fold a miter in the binding; take a stitch or two in the fold to secure it. Then stitch the binding in place up to the next corner. Finish each corner in the same manner.

mitering borders

To add a border with mitered corners, first pin a border strip to a quilt top edge, matching the center of the strip and the center of the quilt top edge. Sew together, beginning and ending the seam 1/4" from the quilt top corners (see Diagram 15).

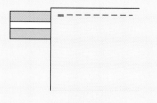

Diagram 15

Allow excess border fabric to extend beyond the edges. Repeat with remaining border strips. Press the seam allowances toward the border strips.

At one corner, lap one border strip over the other (see Diagram 16).

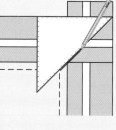

Diagram 16

Align the edge of a 90° right triangle with the raw edge of the top strip so the long edge of the triangle intersects the border seam in the corner. With a pencil, draw along the edge of the triangle from the seam out to the raw edge. Place the bottom border strip on top and repeat marking process.

With the right sides together, match the marked seam lines and pin (see Diagram 17).

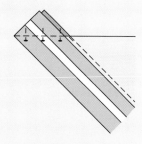

Diagram 17

Beginning with a backstitch at the inside corner, sew together the strips, stitching exactly on the marked lines. Check the right side to see that the corner lies flat. Trim the excess fabric, leaving a 1/4" seam allowance. Press the seam open. Mark and sew the remaining corners in the same manner.

Quick Reference Chart
DIAGONAL MEASUREMENTS OF SQUARES

Use this chart to determine quilt center size of a diagonally set quilt. For example, if blocks finish 12" and are set on point, quilt center size = (17" × number of blocks horizontally) + (17" × number of blocks vertically). To calculate the finished diagonal measurement of a block, multiply finished block measurement (without seam allowances) by 1.414. Shown below are diagonal measurements for several standard block sizes. Figures are rounded up to the nearest ⅛" (.125").

Finished Block Size	Finished Diagonal Measurement	Decimal Equivalent of Diagonal Measurement
1"	1½"	1.5"
1½"	2⅛"	2.125"
2"	2⅞"	2.875"
2½"	3⅝"	3.625"
3"	4¼"	4.25"
3½"	5"	5.0"
4"	5⅝"	5.625"
4½"	6⅜"	6.375"
5"	7⅛"	7.125"
5½"	7⅞"	7.875"
6"	8½"	8.5"
6½"	9¼"	9.25"
7"	10"	10.0"
7½"	10⅝"	10.625"
8"	11⅜"	11.375"
8½"	12⅛"	12.125"
9"	12¾"	12.75"
9½"	13½"	13.5"
10"	14¼"	14.25"
10½"	14⅞"	14.875"
11"	15⅝"	15.625"
11½"	16⅜"	16.375"
12"	17"	17.0"
12½"	17¾"	17.75"
13"	18½"	18.5"
14"	19⅞"	19.875"
15"	21¼"	21.25"
16"	22⅝"	22.625"
17"	24⅛"	24.125"
18"	25½"	25.5"
19"	26⅞"	26.875"
20"	28⅜"	28.375"

Tips for Cutting Borders

- Always cut on the straight grain of the fabric, never on the bias, because the bias has give, and borders with give will cause the quilt to stretch out of shape over time.

- Cut the borders on the lengthwise grain (parallel to the selvage) if you have enough fabric. If cut from a single piece of fabric they will not need to be seamed and will rarely stretch.

- If you must cut the borders on the crosswise grain (perpendicular to the selvage) and seam them, sew them together with diagonal seams, which will be less visible. Borders cut on the crosswise grain have a bit more give and stretch than those cut on the lengthwise grain, and may stretch or sag over time.

Quick Reference Chart
MAGIC NUMBERS FOR ROTARY CUTTING

To determine the cutting size of a variety of shapes when rotary-cutting, use this chart. All measurements assume a ¼" seam allowance is being used.

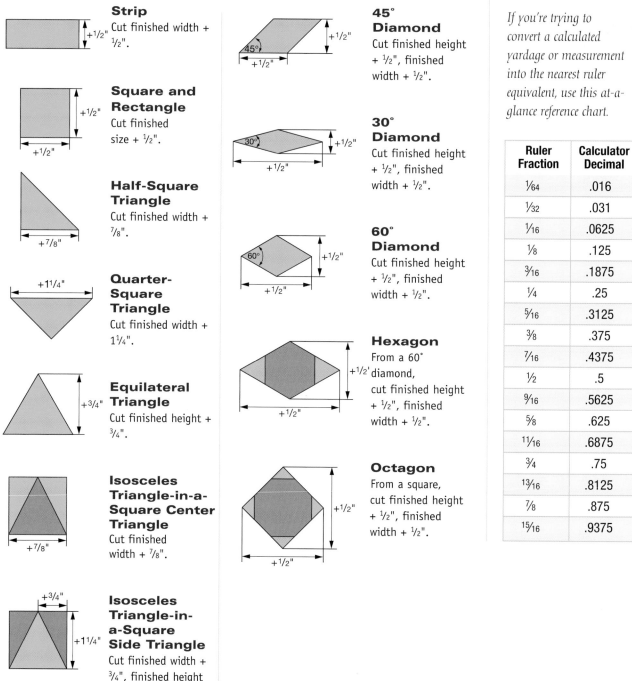

Strip
Cut finished width + ½".

Square and Rectangle
Cut finished size + ½".

Half-Square Triangle
Cut finished width + ⅞".

Quarter-Square Triangle
Cut finished width + 1¼".

Equilateral Triangle
Cut finished height + ¾".

Isosceles Triangle-in-a-Square Center Triangle
Cut finished width + ⅞".

Isosceles Triangle-in-a-Square Side Triangle
Cut finished width + ¾", finished height + 1¼" (must be made in mirror images).

45° Diamond
Cut finished height + ½", finished width + ½".

30° Diamond
Cut finished height + ½", finished width + ½".

60° Diamond
Cut finished height + ½", finished width + ½".

Hexagon
From a 60° diamond, cut finished height + ½", finished width + ½".

Octagon
From a square, cut finished height + ½", finished width + ½".

If you're trying to convert a calculated yardage or measurement into the nearest ruler equivalent, use this at-a-glance reference chart.

Ruler Fraction	Calculator Decimal
¹⁄₆₄	.016
¹⁄₃₂	.031
¹⁄₁₆	.0625
⅛	.125
³⁄₁₆	.1875
¼	.25
⁵⁄₁₆	.3125
⅜	.375
⁷⁄₁₆	.4375
½	.5
⁹⁄₁₆	.5625
⅝	.625
¹¹⁄₁₆	.6875
¾	.75
¹³⁄₁₆	.8125
⅞	.875
¹⁵⁄₁₆	.9375

Quick Reference Chart
YARDAGE WIDTH CONVERSION

If the width of your fabric is different than what the pattern calls for, use this chart to determine the yardage needed.

Yardage conversions are from 44/45"-wide fabric to 36"- or 58/60"-wide fabrics.

44/45"-wide	36"-wide	58/60"-wide	44/45"-wide	36"-wide	58/60"-wide
⅛ yd.	¼ yd.	⅛ yd.	4⅜ yd.	5½ yd.	3⅓ yd.
¼ yd.	⅓ yd.	¼ yd.	4½ yd.	5⅝ yd.	3½ yd.
⅓ yd.	½ yd.	⅓ yd.	4⅝ yd.	5⅞ yd.	3⅝ yd.
⅜ yd.	½ yd.	⅓ yd.	4¾ yd.	6 yd.	3⅝ yd.
½ yd.	⅝ yd.	½ yd.	5 yd.	6¼ yd.	3⅞ yd.
⅝ yd.	⅞ yd.	½ yd.	5⅛ yd.	6½ yd.	4 yd.
⅔ yd.	⅞ yd.	⅝ yd.	5¼ yd.	6⅝ yd.	4 yd.
¾ yd.	1 yd.	⅝ yd.	5⅜ yd.	6¾ yd.	4⅛ yd.
⅞ yd.	1⅛ yd.	⅔ yd.	5½ yd.	6⅞ yd.	4¼ yd.
1 yd.	1¼ yd.	⅞ yd.	5⅝ yd.	7⅛ yd.	4⅓ yd.
1⅛ yd.	1½ yd.	⅞ yd.	5¾ yd.	7¼ yd.	4⅜ yd.
1¼ yd.	1⅝ yd.	1 yd.	6 yd.	7½ yd.	4⅝ yd.
1⅓ yd.	1⅔ yd.	1⅛ yd.	6⅛ yd.	7⅔ yd.	4¾ yd.
1⅜ yd.	1¾ yd.	1⅛ yd.	6¼ yd.	7¾ yd.	4⅞ yd.
1½ yd.	1⅞ yd.	1¼ yd.	6⅜ yd.	8 yd.	4⅞ yd.
1⅝ yd.	2⅛ yd.	1¼ yd.	6½ yd.	8⅛ yd.	5 yd.
1⅔ yd.	2⅛ yd.	1⅓ yd.	6⅝ yd.	8⅓ yd.	5⅛ yd.
1¾ yd.	2¼ yd.	1⅓ yd.	6¾ yd.	8½ yd.	5⅛ yd.
1⅞ yd.	2⅜ yd.	1½ yd.	7 yd.	8¾ yd.	5⅓ yd.
2 yd.	2½ yd.	1⅝ yd.	7⅛ yd.	9 yd.	5½ yd.
2⅛ yd.	2⅔ yd.	1⅝ yd.	7¼ yd.	9⅛ yd.	5½ yd.
2¼ yd.	2⅞ yd.	1¾ yd.	7⅜ yd.	9¼ yd.	5⅝ yd.
2⅓ yd.	3 yd.	1⅞ yd.	7½ yd.	9⅜ yd.	5¾ yd.
2⅜ yd.	3 yd.	1⅞ yd.	7⅝ yd.	9⅝ yd.	5⅞ yd.
2½ yd.	3⅛ yd.	2 yd.	7¾ yd.	9¾ yd.	6 yd.
2⅝ yd.	3¼ yd.	2 yd.	8 yd.	10 yd.	6⅛ yd.
2⅔ yd.	3⅓ yd.	2⅛ yd.	8⅛ yd.	10¼ yd.	6¼ yd.
2¾ yd.	3½ yd.	2⅛ yd.	8¼ yd.	10⅓ yd.	6⅓ yd.
2⅞ yd.	3⅝ yd.	2¼ yd.	8⅜ yd.	10½ yd.	6⅜ yd.
3 yd.	3¾ yd.	2⅓ yd.	8½ yd.	10⅝ yd.	6½ yd.
3⅛ yd.	4 yd.	2⅜ yd.	8⅝ yd.	10⅞ yd.	6⅝ yd.
3¼ yd.	4⅛ yd.	2½ yd.	8¾ yd.	11 yd.	6¾ yd.
3⅜ yd.	4¼ yd.	2⅝ yd.	9 yd.	11¼ yd.	6⅞ yd.
3½ yd.	4⅜ yd.	2⅔ yd.	9⅛ yd.	11½ yd.	7 yd.
3⅝ yd.	4⅝ yd.	2¾ yd.	9¼ yd.	11⅝ yd.	7⅛ yd.
3¾ yd.	4¾ yd.	2⅞ yd.	9⅜ yd.	11¾ yd.	7⅛ yd.
3⅞ yd.	4⅞ yd.	3 yd.	9½ yd.	11⅞ yd.	7¼ yd.
4 yd.	5 yd.	3⅛ yd.	9⅝ yd.	12 yd.	7⅓ yd.
4⅛ yd.	5¼ yd.	3¼ yd.	9¾ yd.	12¼ yd.	7½ yd.
4¼ yd.	5⅓ yd.	3¼ yd.	10 yd.	12½ yd.	7⅝ yd.

index

index continued

quilter's primer